Reviving Main Street

Articles by

Jacques Dalibard

John Edwards

Gordon Fulton

Hans Honegger

Peter Hyndman

Robert Inwood

Harold Kalman

Don Macintosh

Jim Mountain

Chris Pelham

John Stewart

Published in association with the Heritage Canada Foundation by

Reviving Main Street

Edited for the
Heritage Canada Foundation by
Deryck Holdsworth

With a Foreword by
Pierre Berton

UNIVERSITY OF TORONTO PRESS
Toronto Buffalo London

© University of Toronto Press 1985
Toronto Buffalo London
Printed in Canada

ISBN 0-8020-2542-0 (cloth)
ISBN 0-8020-6556-2 (paper)

Canadian Cataloguing in Publication Data

Main entry under title:
Reviving Main Street

Includes index.
ISBN 0-8020-2542-0 (bound).
ISBN 0-8020-6556-2 (pbk.)

1. Central business districts – Canada –
Addresses, essays, lectures.
I. Holdsworth, Deryck, 1947–
II. Heritage Canada.

HT178.C2R48 1985   307.7'6'0971   C85-098392-4

Contents

Foreword

When the Heritage Canada Foundation was launched in 1973, its terms of reference were clear: to work to preserve the built environment of Canada.

Then what is the foundation doing in small towns, holding street fairs, teaching merchants the art of window-dressing, organizing associations of businessmen, worrying about opening and closing hours, parking, and signage?

The answer is simple. It is no use preserving a building unless a use can be found for it. It is no use preserving a streetscape if it is not economically viable. To save the main streets of Canada, the foundation realized it must help to make them pay.

This is a relatively new approach to preservation, but it is the only one that works. For years we tried to save worthy edifices by turning them into museums. The problem was, however, that the cores of small Canadian towns were themselves becoming museum pieces – fossilized buildings, many in disrepair, unable to compete with the massive shopping centre on the outskirts, sucking the life-blood from the main drag.

Yet Main Street is the glory of Canada. If a community has no heart, it has no soul; and its heart should beat faster at the core. For here is the glory of the past, the symbol of stability, the structures that our fathers and their fathers erected, the visual reminder of another time that gives every small town a sense of continuity.

We forget sometimes that Main Street itself is a shopping centre and that by borrowing the techniques of the shopping centre, it can be made to come alive. For Main Street has one advantage: it belongs to the community in a way that the shopping centre, with its franchised outlets, can never belong. The businesses are local ones; the merchants, often, are the sons of those who came before.

Each Main Street is unique because it was developed gradually from within, not imposed suddenly from without. If it has deteriorated, it has deteriorated slowly; thus, its revitalization must also be incremental. Sudden change, forced upon the community, often brings unexpected and devastating results. This is the Heritage Canada philosophy: to preserve the living past through the revitalization of the main streets of the nation; and to do it slowly, through local endeavour and local initiative. The foundation can be the catalyst; it cannot, by itself, be a saviour.

Since the Main Street program was launched a few years ago, the foundation has developed techniques and models through its seven pilot projects in British Columbia, Alberta, Saskatchewan, Ontario, and Nova Scotia. Now the time has arrived to move into the second stage of the program, to 'teach the teachers,' in the words of Jacques Dalibard. The plan is ambitious: to train scores, perhaps hundreds, of Main Street co-ordinators, who can work with business associations and town councils in all ten provinces to preserve this country's built environment.

It is an ambitious project but a worthy one. If it is successful, it will revitalize the face of Canada.

PIERRE BERTON

Preface

In a country as varied as Canada, with its different regional histories, often unique provincial approaches to programs, and no strong federal mandate for heritage or urban affairs, the development of a coherent nation-wide policy for preservation planning is extremely difficult. The Heritage Canada Foundation through its activities has established a strong claim to being the national instrument for the articulation of such a policy. This book has grown out of the foundation's efforts to develop an approach to the revitalization of Main Street, one that can be applied all across Canada in many kinds of communities.

In Nelson, British Columbia; Fort Macleod, Alberta; Moose Jaw, Saskatchewan; Cambridge and Perth, Ontario; and Windsor and Bridgetown, Nova Scotia, from 1981 to 1985 Heritage Canada Foundation co-ordinators helped property owners and merchants on Main Street to become more effective competitors in the age of shopping malls. In these endeavours they were not promoting the prettification of Main Street; they were encouraging communities to restore the life that was already there, by working with the people who were already there. Regional traditions persist in Canada, despite all the standardizing trends of modern economy and modern design. The co-ordinators worked to ensure that nationally useful preservation priorities would be calibrated and adjusted sensitively for local needs and capacities.

The experience of these co-ordinators is presented in this book, not community by community but through the kinds of activities that were found essential in all the demonstration towns – organizing for change, paying attention to the appearance of buildings, thinking about the appropriate signs for store-fronts, encouraging sympathetic new design, upgrading merchants' retailing skills, and promoting downtown as a place to shop. In addition to the co-ordinators' insights there are essays on the past glory and the recent problems of Main Street, on similar programs across Canada, and on the Main Street program in the international context of preservation.

This book has evolved over a number of years. Some six years ago preservation consultant Harold Kalman was commissioned by the Heritage Canada Foundation to prepare a report on Canada's main streets, identifying their serious contemporary problems as well as celebrating their historical identities. That report served as background for the Heritage Canada staff and administration as they began to shape their perspective on the issue of Main Street revitalization. In 1983 John Stewart, then the director of the Main Street program, asked me to integrate Kalman's manuscript with the ideas and experiences accumulated by Heritage Canada through several years of actual field work. At two workshops held in the Ontario communities of Cambridge and Scarborough in the fall of 1983, the co-ordinators shared ideas and problems from their own communities; then, over the following winter, they wrote on the aspects of the program with which they were particularly familiar. Jacques Dalibard, John Stewart, and John Edwards of the foundation's head office in Ottawa contributed essays that define Heritage Canada's approach in comparison with other countries' efforts and with various Canadian provincial initiatives. In the summer of 1984 the manuscript was reviewed and revised by the contributors, by the new Main Street director, François Leblanc, and by Jack Mackenzie, the new chairman of the board of the Heritage Canada Foundation.

The second, more ambitious phase of the Main Street program is about to start, involving some seventy communities over the next half-decade. The members of the first-phase team will be passing on their information not just through this volume but also in their new capacity as regional co-ordinators.

The list of people who have helped to bring this manuscript to fruition would take many paragraphs. Countless provincial and municipal officials, merchants, and corporate representatives unselfishly offered facts, figures, program updates, and opinions. They will recognize their contribution, and the authors and I thank them all. My personal thanks are also owed to Pierre Berton, for generously writing a foreword, and to Prudence Tracy and Susan Kent of University of Toronto Press for their wise counsel in the final stages of writing and publication.

DERYCK HOLDSWORTH

Part One

Louiseville, Quebec

HAROLD KALMAN

Canada's Main Streets

One-fifth of Canada's population live in communities of twenty-five thousand or fewer, and more than one-third in places under fifty thousand. For most of these people Main Street is the physical, commercial, and social heart of their town. Even with the advent of television, mass tourism, and greater daily mobility, Main Street still functions as the heart of their world. Here are the stores, the services, the restaurants, and the social clubs, as well as important public buildings such as the post office and the town hall. Here too are the shop-keepers, bankers, lawyers, and insurance agents with their generation or two of familiarity with the town and their clients. Over some stores are residences; over others, meeting-halls where the Oddfellows or exercise classes or film societies meet.

The street's commercial functions are announced in signs that span the store-front, hang out over the sidewalk, or stand on roof-tops. Signs tell of local names and local businesses. Some names are bracketed by logos for soft-drink or cigarette companies, sewing-machine brands, or appliance makers. Others advertise membership in associations of independent druggists, hardware merchants, or grocers. Rarely are signs or the letters on them all the same age, size, material, or colour. They serve as lines in an ongoing script for the evolving fortunes of Main Street. Behind such signs, buildings of varied size, shape, and appearance similarly record the aspirations and achievements of several generations of merchants and townspeople who have worked on Main Street.

If few of the stores and few of the buildings look identical in the same town, it is also tempting to say that few main streets across Canada

look the same. They have a uniqueness that reflects the different pace
at which commerce developed, capital was invested, and consumers responded. And yet main streets have a familiarity and a similarity
that has prompted a variety of commentators to summarize their essential characteristics. In *Canada* (1964), a portrait composed in collabora-
tion with the photographer Peter Varley, Kildare Dobbs characterized
these places as 'Friendsville, Canada' – the town with several general
stores, a hardware store, a drugstore, two banks, three churches, and
the short-order restaurant. Stephen Leacock, writing before the First
World War, offered his Mariposa (inspired by Ontario's Orillia) as the
model small town. 'I don't know if you know Mariposa,' he wrote. 'If
not, it is of no consequence, for if you know Canada at all, you are
probably well acquainted with a dozen towns like it.' Its landmarks were
clearly defined:

On the Main Street itself are a number of buildings of extraordinary im-
portance. Smith's Hotel and the Continental and the Mariposa House, and the
two banks (the Commercial and the Exchange), to say nothing of McCarthy's
Block (erected in 1878); and Glover's Hardware Store with the Oddfellows Hall
above it. Then on the 'cross' street that intersects Missinaba Street at the main
corner there is the Post Office and the Fire Hall and the Young Men's Christian
Association and the office of the Mariposa Newspacket *– in fact, to the eye of*
discernment a perfect jostle of public institutions comparable only to Thread-
needle Street or Lower Broadway.

For Leacock as for the proud citizens who had erected them, the buildings of small-town Canada and the institutions they housed were one.
The cornice of the Victorian business block provided an architectural
umbrella for local society. Leacock's reference to London's Threadneedle
Street (home of the Bank of England) and New York's Broadway may
be gently ironic, but still it captures the viewer's sense of a miniature
world, the big city writ small but no less impressive. The hotels were a
place for outsiders, especially travelling businessmen, to stay a night
or a week; but their bars and dining-rooms were also reputable places
for all to eat and to socialize. Unlike today's commercial hotels out near
an airport strip or in a motel row on the edge of town, the hotel was
traditionally in the heart of downtown and had noticeable architectural
merit. Stores, not mere one-storey boxes, had as their upstairs neighbours some of the important social institutions of the community. Their
overall mass echoed the requisite big-city images.
   The traditional use of the street as a social space, a meeting ground,
defined the importance of Main Street. In many places Main Street

Main Street has always been the social heart of Canada, the place where people meet, greet, and celebrate, as they do here at the 1914 Dominion Day parade in Vulcan, Alberta.

To the people and their public representatives, 'mainstreeting' has traditionally been a relaxed and informal way of maintaining contact. Here, Governor General Edward Schreyer meets the citizens of Nelson, British Columbia.

served the whole community on Dominion Day, the first of July. In Anglo-Canada, until the last decade or so, Orangemen would march on 12 July under a banner strung across Main Street proclaiming 'In God We Trust.' In Quebec and Acadia, Rue principale was the parade route during the Fête de Pâques. In countless mining towns the march along Main Street to the union hall or the picnic ground celebrated the first of May. Clearly, then, Main Street was a place to witness and be witnessed. As a result, in many communities Remembrance Day parades naturally seek out Main Street, and the various war memorials erected through the last century have a location on or very near Main Street. Similarly, funeral processions often enter into the tradition of public witness by choosing a Main Street route. But always, beyond its memorial function, the street has continued to play a dynamic role. Parades for Santa Claus, St Patrick, pioneer days, and the like find a natural stage along the sidewalks of Main Street. And during election campaigns, here is a natural place to go 'mainstreeting.'

In every region of Canada, Main Street has a particular character. The distinctions came about because of the various ways in which towns were formed, the building materials that were available, the trees that grew best (or were most liked), the predominant social values, and the type of rural economy that lay beyond the town. Many of those distinctions have persisted even though the economic base of the community has changed or the shopping patterns of people have modified. In large part this is due to the longevity of the building stock. Store-front windows and their signs may have changed, but the broader silhouettes remain largely the same. With the important exceptions dealt with in the following chapter, the history of building on Main Street is by and large a pre-Depression activity. It is appropriate, therefore, in trying to define the essence of Main Street, that attention be given to some of the historical forces that contribute to today's visual delight on Main Street.

In the older provinces, Main Street was often a town's name for that portion of a long highway that passed through its limits. It might be called King Street (or Queen Street, if the town was founded during Queen Victoria's reign). In Quebec and Acadia, Rue principale often took its name from the church in that parish (such as Boulevard St-Pierre in Caraquet, New Brunswick). In western Canada, the name of a pioneer landowner or town builder was often used: in Brandon it is Rosser Avenue (after the then chief engineer of the Canadian Pacific Railway); in Nelson it is Baker Street (after a prominent Kootenay landowner). The road was often a transportation route that paralleled an important geographical feature (the sea coast in Nova Scotia or the

St Lawrence River in Quebec) or else had been cut through wilderness by surveyors to provide a route for new settlers (particularly common in Ontario). Towns along this route built their commercial and community buildings in a cluster, often at a major intersection, and private homes were erected farther out along the same road. Trees were planted in front of the residences, and in time these stately rows grew to provide a leafy gateway to the town's commercial centre. Lesser roads would be laid out running perpendicular and parallel to Main Street, and more streets (usually named after local families, politicians, or trees) would be built as the town grew. The result was a gridiron plan, with a rectangular form to the town in Anglo-Canada, a more linear form dominant in French-heritage communities.

Local administrative systems often determined which buildings received the choicest sites. In Quebec and in Acadian parts of the Maritimes, the parish church and the rectory always occupied the prime spot on the street. In other parts of the Maritimes it would be the county hall or the town hall; in Ontario, the town hall and the courthouse. Churches, outside of Quebec, were usually built a few blocks away from the commercial centre. The towns of the West often gave the place of honour to the railway station; indeed, Main Street often ran at right angles to the tracks. Main Street in Moose Jaw, Saskatchewan, for example, terminates at the CPR station.

A few Canadian towns were fully planned from the start, before settlement began. Some exceptional towns received elaborate geometric schemes: Charlesbourg, Quebec, and its neighbour Bourg-Royal were given radial plans in the seventeenth century under the direction of the king of France; Goderich, Ontario, laid out in 1827 for the Canada Land Company by John Galt, has a radial central section (whose core is called the Square, even though it is octagonal) and gridiron beyond. Planned western towns, such as Beiseker, Alberta, formed in 1910 by the Calgary Colonization Company, had more conventional gridiron arrangements. Whatever their shape, these communities were the early precursors of the modern-day tract, except that they contained a full range of uses and not only houses. When mining- or forest-industry companies established townsites for their company workers, they increasingly sought to define social values for their cores; this was in sharp contrast to the saloon and hotel image that dominated in earlier gold- and silver-rush communities. In pulp towns such as Corner Brook, Newfoundland, established by British interests in the 1920s, or Iroquois Falls in Ontario, a church still acts as focus for the treed Main Street. The mill, although clearly the reason for the community's existence, stands at a distance from the town.

Rue principale in St-André-Avellin, Quebec, leads directly to the parish church, the prime symbol of authority in most Quebec towns. The stores along the street are clearly subordinate.

top An impressive clock tower rising above the town hall and fire station in Perth, Ontario, draws attention and life to the centre of town.

bottom Two older landmarks lend substance to a row of commercial buildings along Bridge Street in Carleton Place, Ontario. The clock tower rises from the imposing former post office and federal building, built in 1891. People now mail their letters at an undistinguished one-storey building across the street.

A row of two-storey brick commercial buildings along Bridge Street in Carleton Place, Ontario, is typical of Upper Canadian main streets. Attached businesses simulate the physical continuity of the 'big city.'

Water Street, St Andrews-by-the-Sea, New Brunswick. The residential character of the detached wooden commercial structures is typical of Maritimes main streets.

Differences in materials and variations of economic base give Main Street a distinctive look from region to region. The Atlantic provinces have traditionally used wood to build a series of detached structures, each contained under its own sloping roof, its small windows set into horizontally boarded walls. An economy historically based on the fisheries and lumbering produced an impressive network of local and regional merchants. They carried out their business in large stores that often doubled as warehouses. Many have survived. Lunenburg, Nova Scotia, for example, still has the Zwickers, Eisenhaurs, and other provisioner-merchants on Montague Street, their signs prominent from the harbour side as well as the street. The same kind of detached structure, its gabled roof suggesting residence as much as store, can be found along the Atlantic and Northumberland Strait shores and up the Saint John Valley, in towns that served the New Brunswick lumbering economy.

Newfoundland, with a few exceptions, does not have a particularly strong Main Street tradition. Most communities had been outports for St John's merchants and, under the truck system, exchanged cod for provisions that they could not grow or make themselves. Since Confederation, with the decline of the merchants and the coming of a rudimentary road network, more grocery stores have appeared, often in low, one-storey buildings in front yards. To this day, however, there are in the outports few bank buildings or other Main Street stores and services that other Canadians even in small places take for granted.

In Quebec and Acadia, the notion of a Main Street takes on a special character. For the most part, rural Quebec society was not a commercial economy. Habitants occupied long, thin lots (rotures) laid out at right angles to the road or river. Farmhouses every two or three hundred yards stretched along the road for miles. Farmers were often their own blacksmiths, butchers, furniture makers, and clothesmakers. Grist mills were among the few processing industries to have a centralizing influence on entire communities. Such a subsistence economy gives rise to few establishments, beyond the farm gate, through which a commercial nucleus or Main Street can be defined. The modern retail and service landscape, if there at all, is sporadic and largely ad hoc in nature. Across from the church there may be a boulangerie, often in a recent extension to a far older house. Similarly, there may now be a caisse populaire for financial needs that were certainly not part of the historic society.

For both Quebec and Acadian fishing villages in the Maritimes, Rue principale is a long string of converted houses, their shop-fronts offering a few groceries, a bit of hardware, skidoos, and such like. The brasserie, caisse populaire, Chevaliers de Colomb, and the always dominant parish church help to articulate what is otherwise a modern strip. Occasionally, where a railroad line has crossed the old côtes, a tavern or a railway hotel injects a more commercial silhouette.

In Quebec, communities near to Montreal or Quebec City, such as Longueuil, St-Lambert, Lévis, and Sorel, have a clearly commercial identity. Otherwise, only the Eastern Townships, where initially British and American settlers introduced a commercial agriculture, present a departure from the church-punctuated strip motif. Compton (birthplace of Louis St Laurent), for example, had eight general stores in 1863 (five located on one corner), two hotels (the Oriental and the Compton), and blacksmiths and wheelwrights. Jean-Baptiste-Moïse St Laurent's general store also acted as the village meeting-place, where men chatted, town-council meetings were held, and, in the upper-storey room, the brothers of the Independent Order of Foresters met.

In Ontario, by contrast, Main Street has a far firmer historical definition. Solid rows of attached structures, in stone or brick, often line the sides of Main Street, simulating the physical continuity of a big city. Ontario's nineteenth-century prosperity, based in part on a grain-exporting economy, meant a far greater flow of capital than was the case in Quebec. The consequent demand for goods and services helped to support small-town merchants and manufacturers. Travelling sales representatives supported commercial hotels. Through the latter part of the century stores were built, rebuilt, and extended. In the late 1880s or at the turn of the century a fire would often lead to major new construction projects, with imposing commercial blocks housing four or more ground-floor tenants. The solidity of these two- and three-storey buildings enclosed the street effectively, making it a comfortably defined space for the activities it hosted.

Prairie towns have a character all their own. Many were born overnight as the railways worked their way westwards. Towns were usually located at eight- to ten-mile intervals, the distance that a farmer could conveniently transport his grain by wagon. Most towns were laid out according to a common plan, as Heather Robertson observes in her 1973 study *Grass Roots*:

Prairie towns all look alike: identical grain elevators, identical banks, identical railway stations, a Main Street that is called Main Street and a road along the tracks called Railway Avenue – when you've seen one, as they say, you've seen them all.

The T-shaped intersection of Main Street and Railway Avenue formed the town's main corner. The streets were wide. Main Street might be a

generous sixty-six or even ninety-nine feet wide (based on the sur-
veyor's sixty-six-foot-long chain) – as wide as the height of a seven- or a
ten-storey building. The lowness of the structures along the street
only served to exaggerate its width. This left plenty of room for the
angled parking so characteristic of western towns.

Prairie surveyors usually numbered the roadways ('streets' in one
direction and 'avenues' in the other). To avoid negative numbers,
First Street had to be at the edge of town. The range of numbers allowed
for new streets – Main Street being at their centre – and reflected a
community's early ambitions. High River, Alberta, has its principal intersection at a modestly selected Fourth Street (now Fourth Avenue) and
Railway Avenue (now West First Street, and commonly called Main
Street). At more ambitious Lacombe and Red Deer, also in Alberta, they
upped the ante and made Fiftieth Street the Main Street. Heady Edmon-
ton called the main drag One Hundredth Street.

Commerical buildings in small Prairie towns were often only a single
storey high, with flat parapets along the front hiding a pitched gable
behind. Just as in Leacock's Mariposa, they were designed to imitate
the flat tops of more substantial structures, only this time the models
were in Winnipeg, farther east in Ontario, or perhaps south in Min-
neapolis or Chicago rather than in London's Threadneedle Street. Many
were wood, some of them stuccoed, and in communities near clay pits
they were of local brick. Trees were rarely planted.

Many British Columbia communities grew chaotically during boom and
bust periods before the Great War. Restricted terrain along mountainous
coastlines, inland valleys, or narrow terraces above lakes necessitated a
variety in street layouts, although the unrelenting straight street of
the gridiron often tried to muscle its way up formidable hills. Building
materials depended much on local availability. In mining towns, tree
stumps and seas of mud were edged by boardwalks and crudely built
plank-wall stores that were occupied by restaurants, bakers, and hardware provisioners and quickly joined by many hotels and saloons.
Phoenix, the major copper-mining centre in the Boundary region from
1892 to its closing in 1919, had twenty-eight saloons, five dance-halls,
and gambling casinos among its retail mix. Most of these communities
imitated the exuberance of sister towns along the American mining
frontier in Colorado, Nevada, and California. Some rural service towns,
such as Creston or Kamloops, were more modest in scale; others with
more ambition, such as Nelson, attracted capital and property that en-
dured long after the demise of the more ephemeral production camps
scattered through the surrounding mountains.

British Columbia–style boom-town architecture is also characteristic

Many Prairie towns were born of and shaped almost overnight by the arrival
of the railways and the settlers they carried. Main Street in tiny Balcarres,
Saskatchewan, runs perpendicular to Railway Avenue and the train tracks. The
low frame and stucco buildings, seemingly too small for the broad street,
are characteristic of the Prairies, as are the boom-town false fronts.

By 1900 the citizens of Nelson, British Columbia, were demonstrating their belief
in the community's future by replacing boom-town façades with buildings of
more durable materials.

of some northern communities. The richness of this heritage is perhaps nowhere more evident than in the transformation of Dawson City in the Yukon Territory. The initial shacks and huts of this Klondike boom town were replaced by ornately decorated hotels, saloons, and stores. King, Queen, and Front streets in particular have preserved a wonderful array of commercial architecture that helps Dawson to retain an important place in the Canadian imagination. More recent resource towns in the Far North are far less ornate. Many of their buildings are prefabricated units. Yet the wide streets of Carcross (short for Cariboo Crossing) or Watson Lake, of Whitehorse or Yellowknife, still present an exciting vista, even if there are pick-up trucks and skidoos rather than horses and buggies outside the Main Street stores.

Although there is a strong regional distinctiveness in Canadian main streets, it is possible to identify important similarities. There are structural and human elements that make Main Street a familiar place no matter what region of Canada the community might be in. These commonalities, often the landmark or anchor features of a Main Street, are explored in the next section.

The Building-Blocks of Main Street

Government Buildings

Walk down the Main Street of a Canadian town and you will likely pass the post office, the town hall, and perhaps a county hall or a courthouse. Constructed by one or another level of government, they offer space for the services which our governments provide; they also make a statement about the dominant place of government in our daily lives. Many of the older structures are opulent landmarks in stone, brick, or marble, finished inside with mahogany, walnut, or oak; others are more modest in scale and materials but equally well designed and sited. All are symbols of power, stability, and sophistication, structures which stand out while respecting the scale and appearance of their privately owned commercial neighbours.

For a country spread thinly over three thousand miles of territory, the accessibility of the federal government on a daily basis has always been a priority. The post office is Canada's most ubiquitous national government service. It is a facility that can be found in almost every town. Many a community dates its origin from the time a post office was established. In the past the post office was a symbol of authority; its prominent clock tower and highly visible location at a main intersection were emphatic statements of the federal presence. Indeed, many large

and medium-sized towns established 'federal buildings' which combined post offices with custom houses and desk space for the Department of Agriculture and other bureaus.

These federal government buildings have always been appreciated as
symbols of power and of wealth. Hector Langevin, the minister of
Public Works in the Macdonald government, asserted in 1886 that a
growing young nation had to have 'public offices on a scale commensurate with the wealth and the extent of the city. It is hardly dignified for
the Dominion to have its public offices in a rented or poor building in
large cities.' Buildings in smaller centres may have been less elaborate
but were still intended to make a statement, in Langevin's words, 'on
a scale commensurate' with the community. Accordingly, federal buildings sprang up from coast to coast bearing clock towers and sculpted
façades intended to mark the time and delight our senses. In so far as
these buildings came from the Department of Public Works, there is a
certain familiarity in their designs from place to place. The Ottawa offices
of a series of chief Dominion architects produced a steady stream of
designs during periods of rapid national expansion.

The provinces' principal presence outside the capital city was originally restricted to the courthouse with its attached jail. (In some provinces courthouses have been built by county governments.) Most courthouses were imposing buildings which expressed the power of the
law and added to the quality of the town; they were usually designed in
a classical mode and built of local materials. The Ontario town of
Cobourg built an impressive pile, Victoria Hall, that served as the town's
assembly rooms as well as the region's courthouse. Opened by the
Prince of Wales in 1860, it was not paid for until 1938. About twenty
districts of Upper Canada had similar, if more modest, courthouses.
More a tradition in the older parts of the country than in the West,
perhaps the most impressive examples east of Ontario can be found in
the old Loyalist-settled areas of the Maritimes. St Andrews and Woodstock, New Brunswick, both boast particularly fine examples.

The most familiar landmark on Main Street may be the town hall. Here
the municipal government flexed its architectural muscles and claimed
its control. The town hall frequently boasts a clock tower – sometimes
the fire department's hose tower in disguise – precociously rivalling
the one erected by the post office. The historical context for these buildings is important. They should not be regarded as the third tier of
government, far behind federal and provincial buildings in importance.
For many communities, the town hall was the most important political
venue of all. This attitude dates back at least to Loyalist days. During the
first half of the nineteenth century the demands for increased local

authority resulted in parliamentary measures which stressed the significance and centrality of municipal government – and municipal buildings. Architectural historian Marion MacRae, in her 1983 study *Cornerstones of Order*, noted the significance of these measures, whereby

*bodies of elected men had the right to build county courthouses, county bridges,
and town or township halls – not by public subscription, but on taxes from a
rateable property – and many proceeded to do so. They leapt at the chance to
convert the dream of many years into the most impressive reality within their
compass.*

The activities to be sheltered by a new town hall could be quite numerous, requiring facilities above and beyond the basic provisions for a
council chamber, offices for the town clerk and other officials, police
office, lock-up, and fire engine and hose space. Often the facilities
included space for a market, held indoors in recognition of the harsh
Canadian winters (or under verandas along the sides of the building,
to be incorporated into later extensions). In many cases, there was also
an assembly hall or ballroom. As a result, the structure could easily be
three storeys high and of considerable square footage, even in seemingly
small communities. Dressed in either the neoclassical or the Gothic
trim of the day, the structure proudly announced the town's sense of
itself. If visitors perchance mistook the local Oddfellows Hall for the
town hall, the council might well vote to upgrade its municipal façade.
The town of Perth felt that its town hall was only really finished once
the cupola and clock tower were added, some eight years after the building was functional.

   Another landmark on many Canadian main streets is the public library.
As in the case of the town hall, the presence of such a structure reflects
local initiative. Although many communities in eastern Canada had
Mechanics Institutes (private libraries) from the first third of the
nineteenth century, municipal responsibility for libraries began in
the 1880s. Between 1901 and 1911 some 125 Canadian communities
(111 of them in Ontario) gained a Carnegie library. In order to qualify
for a grant from the Carnegie Foundation, established by Pittsburgh
steel magnate Andrew Carnegie after he sold his vast industrial
empire, a municipality had to guarantee to raise from taxes an annual
amount for library maintenance equivalent to one-tenth the grant.
Usually rather homey places, one storey high, they had sufficient
classical trim to be eye-catching and dignified without being overly
ostentatious.

Beyond the capital cities, the local courthouse has been the principal expression of the provincial presence. This fanciful courthouse in Nelson, British Columbia, was built in 1907–9 to a design by the renowned F.M. Rattenbury.

Often the most imposing buildings in small towns are those that housed federal government activities. In Arnprior, Ontario, the former federal building is now a library and museum.

The theatre, the auditorium, and the opera house on Main Street have meant a great deal to the life of Canadian communities. This large and elegant auditorium occupies the upper floor of the town hall in Carleton Place, Ontario. It is rarely used today.

The Carnegie library in Perth, Ontario, built in 1909 from standardized plans

The prefabricated Bank of Commerce in Watson, Saskatchewan, erected 28 November 1906. The significance of the prefab banks, designed in Toronto and manufactured in Vancouver, has been recognized by the federal Historic Sites and Monuments Board: its plaque can be seen to the left of the entrance.

Commerical Buildings

It would be understandable if a stranger, looking for the town hall or post office, gravitated instead to one of the banks on Main Street. Especially when they occupy corner sites, banks provide one of the most noticeable design elements – not to mention functional linchpins – in almost any Canadian community.

Canada, it sometimes appears, is a nation of banks. Our banking system created a small oligarchy of federally chartered banks which are allowed to operate from coast to coast. All have built an enormous network of branches. In Canada's early years a large number of banks vied for the public's money and business. Many were unincorporated banks, locally owned and managed family businesses – providing a credit system that linked overseas trade in cod, timber, or wheat with stores that served the local population. These often operated from the lower floor of the family home or warehouse. Changes in the Bank Act at the end of the nineteenth century led to a wave of take-overs. Regional banks in Ontario and Quebec became national banks, operating from coast to coast; they opened up new branches or took over the smaller operations that had previously served parts of the Maritimes or the Eastern Townships or parts of Ontario.

Competition and common sense led the banks to project an image of stability and security in their buildings in order to win confidence and attract deposits. Big-city banks predictably turned to the forms of Greek and Roman architecture: after all, what could be more stable and more impressive than a classical temple that had been around for two thousand years? Establishing branches in the small towns, however, posed more of a problem. Few small towns had architects, and it took time for head office to respond to the call for a new branch. Yet speed was essential. As the population and the economy surged west and north, the banks struggled to gain initial control of the markets by being the first in town.

How was a bank to build quickly yet imposingly? The best solution came from the Canadian Bank of Commerce. Between 1906 and 1910 the British Columbia Mills, Timber, and Trading Company of Vancouver supplied the Commerce with some seventy prefabricated 'Prairie-type' banks in three sizes, designed by the prestigious Toronto architectural firm of Darling and Pearson. Knocked-down banks in three- and four-foot-wide wooden wall sections were sent through the mountains by train. Once at their destination the buildings could be assembled in a day. The Commerce staffed its many new branches (149 in the West in ten years) by recruiting young clerks in Scotland. The directors were proud that their new banks were elegant, handsomely clad in wooden pilasters and pediments. Handsome as they were, the banks did not dominate the rather crudely built boom-town fronts of their neighbours.

Other banks were also committed at an early date to designing branches from a central location. The Eastern Townships Bank (later part of the Commerce) did so in eastern Quebec in the 1870s. Similarly, the Bank of Nova Scotia retained architect John M. Lyle in the 1920s and 1930s to produce plans for banks both large and small.

If the banks are the specialty commercial building on Main Street, many other enterprises are housed in what might be called commercial buildings. Many of these were originally built as detached structures, perhaps even consisted of converted houses – a doctor's home might house an apothecary in the front room, for example. Rebuilt when space became cramped, such businesses then acquired a more urban appearance of store front, façade, and cornice. Often, whole commercial blocks were built after fire destroyed the business section of a town. Merchants in commercial blocks would lease space from the property owners or, if profits had been good, perhaps become the landlords themselves. In many communities, the Oddfellows, Foresters, or Freemasons were building owner or upstairs tenant. Pediments and elaborate cornices served as umbrella for commerce and fraternity.

The range of goods offered on a Main Street depended upon the size of the community and the trading hinterland that it could carve out for itself. In many Ontario communities that economic base might sustain several blocks of one street, or even secondary retail streets. For small Prairie hamlets, no more than eight or ten miles from their competitors, one side of one street might contain all the shops in sight. Waskada, Manitoba, for example, had a population of 250 in 1916. Within 250 feet along Railway Avenue, across from three grain elevators, could be found three automobile showrooms or repair garages, a harness shop, two confectioners, two general stores, two hardware stores, a bank, a furniture store, and a drugstore. Rounding out the retail mix, along First and Second streets, were a baker, two barber shops, two pool halls, a Chinese laundry, a Women's Christian Temperance Union restaurant, three implement dealers, a telephone office, and the council office. Apart from the bank and two other buildings in stone, all were one- or two-storey wooden structures with false-front façades.

In the early decades of this century retailing patterns were already beginning to change. Individuality persisted, but ownership began to be less local. Some independent grocers failed, while others were bought out by better-capitalized merchants. Nearly a century ago grocers Robert

Kelly of Vancouver and James Albert MacDonald of Winnipeg began acquiring grocery stores and food-processing plants and setting up distribution centres. Their operations grew to become the large Super-Valu (Kelly-Douglas) and MacDonald Consolidated supermarket chains. They in turn were swallowed up by the even larger Weston's (Loblaws) and Safeway chains. And so it was with many other lines of trade. Cunningham and Koffler developed drugstore chains in British Columbia and Ontario respectively; today all are part of the latter's Shoppers Drug Mart chain, itself part of a larger operation. Imasco Ltd of Montreal, which owns Shoppers, recently bought Peoples Drug Inc, an American operation with six hundred stores in the United States. Shoppers is now the fourth-largest drug chain in North America.

Timothy Eaton, the father of the department store in Canada, opened a small store at Toronto's Yonge and Queen streets in 1869. His innovations included the elimination of bargaining and barter, and the privilege of exchanging unsatisfactory goods. Within a decade, the business had grown into a full-fledged department store with a wide range of merchandise. The T. Eaton Company expanded to Winnipeg in 1905 and was in eight provinces by 1930, when it rang up a staggering 7 per cent of Canada's retail trade. One critical device for attaining that market share was its mail-order catalogue operation, which put all the variety of a major department store into rural consumers' backyards. Mail-order outlets numbered 74 in Ontario, 111 nation-wide, by 1930, many in small towns. Eatons also introduced groceterias on to Main Street, especially in Ontario. A precursor of self-service supermarkets, the groceteria displayed tins and packages of food on shelves along aisles. A clerk at the front of the store calculated the price totals.

While Eatons would gradually move off Main Street into regional malls, another famous retailer, Woolworth's, has remained a landmark in many small communities. In 1879, at the age of twenty-six, Frank Winfield Woolworth opened his first 'Great 5¢ Store' in Utica, New York. The Utica store lasted less than four months, but in the following years Woolworth opened many long-lived retail outlets through the American northeast. Twelve were in operation in 1889, 54 in 1899, and 238 in 1909. Woolworth provided several important innovations in his very first store: all merchandise was sold at one fixed price – five cents; all goods were arranged on the counters, where the customers could see and handle them; and all purchases were for cash, not credit. The five-cent line was soon supplemented by a ten-cent and then a fifteen-cent counter. The chain sought locations in communities of twenty thousand or more people. It proved that centralized mass buying could provide the customer with good values.

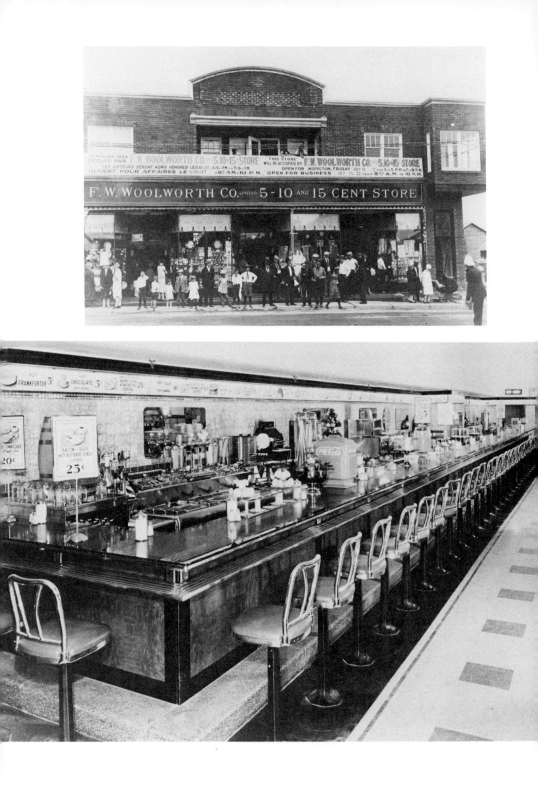

top Woolworth's, a familiar presence on Main Street, arrives in Jonquière, Quebec, 16 July 1927.

Towns with populations as small as one thousand people often had movie theatres on Main Street. The Empress Theatre in Fort Macleod, Alberta, has been reborn as a performing-arts centre and movie house.

bottom The Woolworth's lunch counter in Montreal, Quebec: elbow to elbow for five-cent hot dogs

The five-and-ten came to Canada in 1897 when S.H. Knox, a cousin and partner of F.W. Woolworth, opened a store in Toronto. Another Woolworth friend and associate, E.P. Charlton, began a store in Montreal soon afterwards. Both the Knox and Charlton chains merged with F.W. Woolworth and Co in 1912, and the Woolworth name has appeared on Canadian store-fronts ever since. Woolworth's expansion in Canada was rapid and continuous. Decisions to build were made at the Toronto head office and ratified by the executive committee in New York. By the late 1940s, the now-familiar yellow brick, aluminum window sashes, green marble 'bulkheads' below the windows, and tile parapets were all prerequisites, as was the interior column spacing of twenty-five feet, designed to accommodate uniform fixtures. Yet Woolworth's always tried to dispel the 'head-office' stigma and to be a good neighbour on Main Street by allowing some flexibility in building height and composition to fit a particular location.

Stedmans is another chain that has stayed on Main Street. Opening their first business, Stedman Brothers' book and stationery store, in 1905 in Brantford, Ontario, George Samuel and Edward Stedman soon added further shops and experimented with manufacturing and wholesaling as well as retailing. Difficulties encountered during the First World War (they were importing and marketing many German-made goods) limited them to acting as 'wholesalers of general merchandise.' The company moved to Toronto in 1924 and returned to the retail business a few years later. It expanded throughout the Depression and again in the 1950s. By 1961 Stedmans had 138 company-owned stores, 200 associated stores, and 200 catalogue accounts, mostly in small towns. A historical sketch of the firm explains its marketing policy:

From 1945 to 1961, unlike many other variety chain stores (e.g., Woolworth's and others), the company's main emphasis was directed towards rural and semi-urban centres of population, because management believed that this rapidly growing market presented unique opportunities. Stedmans believed that competitive prices, dependable quality and personal service – rather than expensive surroundings and heavy advertising – were the keys to successful merchandising in the variety store industry.

Stedmans has continued where Woolworth's left off, by directing its attention to small communities and by remaining committed to staying on Main Street. The firm's first market is towns of five to ten thousand persons, and it has recently turned towards those of up to twenty thousand. The Stedman name appears on about sixty company-owned stores and more than two hundred franchise locations. The company's letterhead describes the firm as 'the family store with the hometown feeling.'

That local, home-town feeling can usually be found by going into a community's Main Street coffee shop, tea-room, or drugstore soda fountain. It is still a place to meet, to pass the time of day, and to catch up on news. Mel's Tea Room in Sackville, New Brunswick, also functions as the waiting-room for the intercity bus lines and the place to buy local papers, lottery tickets, and locally produced maple syrup.

There is one further activity, also leisure related, that is a familiar Main Street fixture – the movie house. The often elegant 1920s and 1930s façades, slightly whimsical, exotic, and surrounded by flashing lights, became another landmark in many towns. Although the theatre was basically a cavernous hall for most of its floorspace, its street entrance and foyer received considerable design attention. Like the other merchants on Main Street, the theatre provided a space where the small-town and rural dweller found that he need not travel to metropolitan centres for a taste of big-city life. And on a snowy winter night, when the movie ends and the lights go out in the movie-house kiosk, then there are still countless places across Canada where Ralph Connor's 1919 sentiment, expressed in *The Settler*, applies:

It was long past midnight. Even Main Street, that most splendid of all Canadian thoroughfares, lay white and spotless and, for the most part, in silence.

A battle-weary merchant vents his frustration in downtown Cambridge, Ontario.

HAROLD KALMAN

Crisis on Main Street

The deterioration of Main Street has proceeded slowly but surely over the last few decades. The unabated spread of suburban and regional shopping malls has siphoned off vitality from town centres and left Main Street with a far smaller share of commerce that it once was accustomed to. The merchants who remain have transformed their buildings with layers of once-trendy materials in the name of modernization. These renovations, often implemented in response to the new malls, have obscured or destroyed the beauties and integrity of the traditional designs and replaced them with a mélange of materials that can only be described as tacky. Equally harmful are the new (and not-so-new) signs – big, bold, and brassy banners that simply use the buildings as a backdrop.

Property owners, encouraged by zoning changes, have hurt themselves yet more by allowing the upper floors of their buildings to become run down and vacant. The loss of residents and office workers has drained a vital part of the life-blood from Main Street and deprived storekeepers of a captive market. The need for customer parking – to match a convenience offered by the mall – led to wholesale change on the street. Curbside parking allows only one or two spaces for every shop. To provide additional stalls, buildings were demolished and parking lots created. The result has been closure of more and more stores, loss of additional residents upstairs, and gaps where once there were continuous rows of buildings.

Further, building authority has steadily become more centralized, resting mainly in the hands of relatively few organizations – particularly retail chains, banks, and government agencies – whose head offices are more concerned with structural efficiency and standardization than with sensitivity to the architectural character of a particular town. Local control, even local input, has been eroded.

Yet, for a long time, nobody seemed to care very much. Main Street found itself becoming a thing of the past. It even received the ultimate insult: being thrust into a museum. Institutions such as the British Columbia Provincial Museum in Victoria and the Western Development Museum in Saskatoon have created 'Main Streets' along which visitors can walk and reminisce. And, of course, the street became that most popular of nostalgic American attractions – Disneyland's 'Main Street, U.S.A.'

Main Street and the Shopping Mall

The shopping mall is the biggest threat to the survival of Main Street. Credit for the first group of stores adjacent to a large parking lot at the edge of town is usually given to the Country Club Plaza, built in 1923 in Kansas City, Missouri. Shopping centres began to appear in number in the United States immediately after the Second World War. They came to Canada in 1949 with the simultaneous building of the Dorval shopping centre near Montreal (inspired by a New York development) and Park Royal in West Vancouver (modelled after one near Seattle). In the three decades that followed, the shopping centre matured into the shopping mall, with stores turning their backs on the parking lot and opening from a fully enclosed, climate-controlled, and activity-filled circulation space. It was called a mall after the traditional sheltered and fashionable promenade; the name derives from the alley in which people played the game of 'mall,' or 'pall mall,' a sport similar to croquet.

Shopping-centre developers usually determine in advance what kind of retailers they want and then go with familiar national tenants. One, two, or three department stores act as anchors; their assured success attracts shoppers to the specialty stores. The chains are known quantities, and they can be recruited easily through their head offices. Trevor Smith, whose Burnac Leaseholds Limited has developed more than one hundred shopping centres across the country, explains that he can lease a proposed mall with only a dozen phone calls. This procedure favours the large chains and hurts independent businesses. Charles Flavelle, who manufactures Vancouver's R.C. Purdy chocolates, recalls how two decades ago he failed to procure an outlet in his own city's Oakridge shopping centre. The national developers chose Laura Secord, a chain popular in Ontario but then virtually unknown in the West.

Village Square in the Scotia Square development in Halifax is an indoor mall that attempts to mimic the human scale of Main Street.

The original Hudson's Bay Company store, built in 1900, in Nelson, British Columbia

OPPOSITE

top The same building modernized in 1935: fresh paint, lowered ceilings, streamlined awnings, and maintenance-free shop-front materials

bottom The Bay building in Nelson as it appears today. The façade has become a signboard, while the structural features and character of the building, hidden under a 1960s modernist shroud, await rediscovery.

Purdy's has itself become a large regional chain and is now welcomed to shopping-centre locations. More than half of the shopping centres in the Atlantic region are owned by non-Atlantic-region developers, according to University of New Brunswick engineer Michael Ircha. Further, more than half of the shopping-centre retailing space is leased to national department and retail chain stores headquartered in Toronto and Montreal. A substantial amount of region-generated profits flow back to corporate head offices. More important, perhaps, is that the merchandise is selected from outside the local area.

Shopping centres discriminate in other ways against independents. The rental rates paid by chains can be as low as half of those paid by their independent competitors. Shopping-centre developers claim that this is partly because chains offer better prospects for success since they can borrow money at the prime rate when even established independents must pay 1 or 2 per cent over prime. National chains are in effect being subsidized by local independents.

The attraction of the shopping mall for the consumer is easy to understand: malls are convenient, and their very predictability is pleasant. The modern mall is designed with fountains, escalators, and other visual and aural features calculated to stimulate – or soothe – the shopper and keep her (85 per cent of customers are women) inside the building. Entrances are well marked from the parking lot, but exits are difficult to find from within. Management generally retains strict control over store hours, signs, and display techniques and co-ordinates promotion, advertising, and special events.

A crucial advantage which the shopping mall holds over the downtown business district is the availability of parking. Vast acres of asphalt ensure that parking spaces are almost always available, even if hundreds of metres away from the stores. Somehow the long walk across the parking lot rarely bothers the shopper, whereas the same walk through several downtown blocks acts as a deterrent.

And inevitably, as shoppers have gravitated towards the shopping mall, many community social events – traditionally the backbone of Main Street – have followed. Even the invention of downtown, the sidewalk sale, has found its way into the shopping centre. In some cases the mall has imitated Main Street, adopting a village theme. A new shopping centre in St-Sauveur, Quebec, resembles a gaudy version of a Québécois town, with steep-roofed shops treated like a randomly sited cluster of houses. In Mississauga, Ontario, Sherwood Village offers 'olde-tyme shopping, the friendly way it used to be' in neo-Tudor shops.

Meanwhile, as the suburbs of large cities became saturated with shopping centres, developers began to put them up by smaller cities and towns. A mammoth regional mall would locate in a rural area within easy driving distance of a number of medium-sized and small communities in a market area sufficiently large to attract major department stores. These shopping centres thus came to compete directly with towns as well as cities. American journalist Calvin Trillin, writing in *New Yorker* magazine in July 1980, described the regional shopping centre incisively after having attended a meeting of the International Council of Shopping Centres:

Regionals are always anchored, as shopping-centre people say, by department stores – usually two and perhaps as many as four or five. A regional's department stores are separated by several dozen smaller stores. A regional is always surrounded by acres of parking. It normally has an enclosed mall ... the formula is so unvarying that once the elements have been set in place ... a well-established developer might pencil in the names of some tenants before he begins negotiating with them, the assumption being that some credit-jewellery chains and shoe chains and clothing chains will put a store in any regional whose developer can produce a projection sheet with acceptable numbers on it. If a regional is not spouting money the way that it was designed to, the developer can adjust what he calls the mix – the way someone running an engine might adjust the fuel mix. In time, he can cut the percentage of shoe stores or increase the percentage of jeans stores.

Trillin characterizes the mall as an invention, a selling machine. He continues by contrasting it to Main Street:

Among the disadvantages a traditional downtown has in trying to meet the competition of a regional ... is the handicap of not being a machine. Nobody owns downtown. Nobody can adjust the mix.

The only blessing may be that peripheral shopping-centre building is on the decline. Developers are having trouble finding new cornfields, as they call their sites. Statistics Canada notes that suburban and regional mall construction has peaked. The International Council of Shopping Centres' Albert Sussman finds the situation the same in the United States: 'There has been a real slowdown. We have been running out of markets for development of new centres.'

If the wave has peaked in most of the country, it is still cresting in Atlantic Canada, the last region to receive a modern network of roads and the last region to feel the impact of shopping centres. John Thorpe, of the Nova Scotia Ministry of Development, calculates that there are enough shopping malls in the province to service a population six times larger than the present 900,000. Typical Maritimes communities contain about three thousand people, and their traditional main streets are having considerable difficulty combating the brand-new malls. Beleaguered merchants have been assisted by new legislation aimed at inhibiting the growth of new regional shopping malls. Nova Scotia, Prince Edward Island, and New Brunswick have all enacted bills to this end in the last few years.

Nova Scotia's Act to Regulate the Development of Shopping Centres states that municipalities within fifty miles of a proposed large shopping centre (50,000 square feet or more) must be notified of the plans and may represent their views at a hearing of the provincial Planning Appeal Board. Moreover, the board is to consider whether the additional retail space is needed or desirable and to determine as well its effect upon existing stores in the area.

Prince Edward Island slapped a moratorium on all shopping centres of more than 6,000 square metres (nearly 65,000 square feet) in 1979 because, as the Speech from the Throne stated, 'the economic and social impact of such development is not ... clear.' A subsequent government-commissioned report on retail-store development confirmed that large regional shopping centres contribute to the business and social decline of small communities and of the downtown areas of larger ones. It recommended that the province control shopping-centre development. As a result of a 1981 amendment to the provincial Planning Act, all applications to build shopping centres larger than 2,000 square metres must be approved by the minister of Community Affairs.

New Brunswick has also controlled shopping-centre development. That province's Community Planning Act says that no shopping centre can be built outside of a municipality without the approval of the provincial government. In 1981 additional legislation required cabinet approval for any proposed centre in excess of 200,000 square feet. The fourth Atlantic province, Newfoundland, has no legislation as yet, but the newly formed Newfoundland Independent Business Association has made shopping-centre control its highest priority in discussions with the government.

The central and western provinces have no direct legislation to control shopping centres, but their Main Street– and downtown-revitalization programs do inhibit shopping-centre growth. Ontario effectively froze peripheral mall development by declaring that new malls required an amendment to the zoning by-law; this in turn necessitated hard-to-acquire approval by adjacent municipalities.

The battle between Main Street and the shopping mall is a continuing one. Main Street has changed in the post-war years as it has struggled

Shoppers are assured of plenty of free parking at the malls in Sydney, Nova Scotia.

to cope with the new reality. Penetration by chains, as merchants became more and more the local representatives of regional or national firms, caused one type of change. A second change occurred when independent merchants as well as the chains, in order to hang the new and modern signs, covered old façades with new materials, such as aluminum siding, that were incompatible with the character of the street. When that happened, Main Street changed architecturally as well as economically.

Chains and Main Street

Regional and national names appear on countless signs along main streets across the country. Canadian Tire, Allied Hardware, People's, Provigo, Mac's Milk, and many other familiar names have a hold upon the nation's retail trade. The fast-food industry is, of course, dominated by chains such as McDonald's, Kentucky Fried Chicken, and St-Hubert BBQ. The chains are everywhere.

The immense buying power of the chains and department stores gives them the leverage to demand large discounts or allowances from manufacturers. The independents, as a result, are continually undersold. Local businesses suffer, and many fail. The concentration and centralization of buying power can also ignore local needs. Chains offer the same standardized merchandise to a broad market. Consumers suffer because they cannot find the goods they want. Cecil Harrison, owner of a 102-year-old general store in Ormond, Ontario, expressed his bitterness towards the chains when he was forced into bankruptcy in 1981. He sent his customers a leaflet with the following poem:

The chain stores all have come to town, it seems they have control.
And it seems a man just doesn't own his body or his soul.
Oh yes, their stores are pretty, and their windows have flash,
But they never know a person, if they haven't got the cash.

The growth of chains has hurt independent businesses in other ways, beyond providing them with stiff competition. The domination of the retail trade by chains has affected the appearance of Main Street as much as it has affected the shopper and the independent retailer. Primary is the chains' desire for standardized outlets. In the interest of efficiency many head offices have produced standardized plans that they feel best accommodate their standard counters and standard fittings, that control traffic in the way best suited to each particular chain's standard merchandising techniques and thus produce a standard image.

King Street East in Hamilton was typical of many fondly remembered
main streets.

When King Street merchants decided to compete by adopting the visual formulas
of the malls, the textures of the past – the awnings and signs of independent
merchants, sidewalk displays, overhead wires – all vanished.

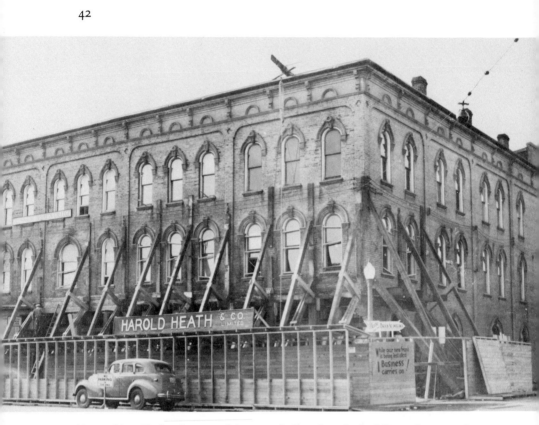

Erected in 1882 by the son of the town's founder, the building taken over by Heath's department store in Tillsonburg, Ontario, was characteristic of the town's commercial buildings, with its brick walls and Italianate arched windows. In 1947 the ground floor was opened up to create large display windows; above, timber shoring supports the walls during these first alterations.

OPPOSITE

top Heath's department store circa 1960: the walls are painted white and a large fascia sign partly obscures the windows.

bottom In 1972 Heath's was given a veneer of featureless white siding. The store's management was motivated by a commendable attempt to save the commercial viability of Broadway; unfortunately, an attractive building was concealed and architectural continuity destroyed in the process. The branch of the Royal Bank of Canada at the right is scheduled to be rebuilt: one change forces another by making the neighbouring buildings seem old-fashioned.

Franchised operations cannot be controlled to the same extent as company-owned stores, but all outlets are designed or influenced to some degree by headquarters. Sometimes all that is demanded is renovation – as with the metal siding so characteristic of franchised Canadian Tire stores. But older buildings often cannot be adapted to meet the company's desired layout and image. As a consequence, pressure arises to tear down existing buildings and replace them with new stores, preferably without second- and third-storey suites or offices that are seen only as a nuisance to rent. The result: the loss of many of Main Street's older structures. In their place rise red and white–striped Kentucky Fried Chicken outlets, pyramid-roofed St-Hubert BBQs, and one-storey Stedman stores with their concrete-block and glass façades. Few are designed with any respect for their neighbours.

The chains' conspicuous signs – which we are forced to notice long before we look at the buildings – have also hurt Main Street. They carry names, logos, and colours that are dictated by head office. Many are enormously overscaled and are fabricated of back-lit plastic to catch the attention of the speeding motorist at any time of the day or night. Modern corporate signs often bear no relationship to the buildings from which they hang; indeed, they often do their best to obscure them. Older structures were usually designed to support simple and narrow fascia signboards across the front over the ground floor, as well as painted or neon signs on or in the windows. The oversized new signs overwhelm their buildings, and their standardized shapes and colours clash with the structures that hold them. Some chains go so far as to hide the upper façades of their buildings entirely behind metal siding that serves as the background for giant billboards. Any sense of harmony once found on Main Street is shattered by this competition to be conspicuous.

A further result is a depressing sameness in towns from one end of the country to another. Every Main Street is laced with structures and signs that could be almost anywhere. Prince Edward Island is becoming just like Saskatchewan. The regional features that have been so much a part of Main Street are eroded. Gone is the continuous fabric of commercial blocks that made the street something special.

A classic example of architectural change can be seen in Tillsonburg, Ontario. Named for its ample hundred-foot width, Broadway is the Main Street of the picturesque town. Broadway's many stores serve the town's ten thousand as well as the large trading area in the three adjacent counties. The largest store in town is Heath's, a junior department store. The family-owned business began in nearby Delhi in 1843, came to Tillsonburg in 1945, and expanded to Woodstock two years later. The store in Tillsonburg leased its retail space in an imposing and attractive Italianate brick building that had been erected in 1882 by E.D. Tillson, youngest son of the town's founder. In 1947 Heath's inserted steel beams and columns to open larger show windows and entrances and updated the building's image by erecting a continuous fascia over the ground floor. The sign was uneven in height to allow light into the second-floor offices at the left of the building.

Twenty years later the company purchased the building from the Tillson estate. Realizing that area shopping centres would add strong competition, management started immediate plans for a major face-lifting. Work was carried out in 1972. Designed Construction of Mississauga, the store's interior designers, conceived and built a new front that completely covers the Broadway façade and wraps around the first part of the wall on the side street. The new façade totally changes the scale and character of the building. It now appears as a modernistic single-storey mass, in absolute contrast with the remarkably uniform smaller-scale Italianate buildings along the rest of the block. The harmony of the streetscape was lost in one fell swoop. In the store's own promotional words, it is now 'the big store on the corner.'

Heath's may have harmed the town from the perspective of architectural continuity, but it gave the community a large and needed boost economically. The motivation, it will be recalled, was to compete with suburban commercial development. This apparently succeeded. R.T. Saxby, Heath's chairman of the board, reports that 'we are delighted with the result and feel sure that in spite of two new shopping centres … we will be able to maintain our position in the community.' The store and its designer believed that the best way Main Street could compete with the shopping centres was to try to look like those centres. In the early 1970s this logic may have seemed irresistible. Old buildings were seldom appreciated and were felt to be a commercial liability. Moreover, the success of shopping centres was then attributed in large part to their design. Now we realize that their prosperity owes more to such factors as management and promotional techniques, uniform hours of opening, and ample parking. Heath's played a positive role in struggling to save Broadway from the competition – but in the process it defaced the very street it hoped to save.

If the chains and the independent merchants transformed Main Street architecture and commerce in the name of modernity and progress, a design change that was perhaps even more devastating came from the banks. The tendency towards centralized and standardized design increased in the decades following the Second World War. The banks built numerous new branches as they sought to regain some of the

losses suffered during the Depression and to replace older branches
which they believed had outlived their usefulness. Efficiency was the
watchword, and the most efficient form of building was a one-storey
rectangular box. Each bank had its own variant – the Commerce and the
Bank of Montreal preferred brick, and the Royal Bank tended towards
black granite. Few related to their neighbours, which were, for the most
part, taller and older structures built of local materials and designed in
the manner of the region. To make matters worse, many older buildings
were swept away to make room for the new banks. A significant
number of these older buildings themselves housed banks. The street
suffered, since, as we have seen, banks used to be landmarks, with
their columns, pediments, and strong design, and were often located on
several corners of the town's key intersection. As in a smile with
several teeth knocked out, gaps appeared at important points on the
street. One-storey boxes dressed in new materials did not fill the
gaps. At the time, no one noticed. In the fifties and early sixties, periods
of vast and sudden change, progress was equated with modernity,
and our physical heritage was all but ignored.

The 11 longest-established chartered banks, mammoth bureaucratic
institutions, do business from some 7,500 branches (up sharply from
5,000 in 1960). In addition to the chartered banks, Canada's 75 trust
companies, 3,600 credit unions and caisses populaires, and 2 provincial
deposit agencies operate a total of 5,800 branches. They too have a
decided architectural presence. As the range of banking services these
agencies provide has expanded, their new buildings are looking more
and more like banks. Indeed, the frequency of new look-alike one-storey
trust-company offices suggests that their designers, in conceptual terms,
are close to where the banks' architects were a decade or two ago.

The impetus for new design (and alterations to existing banks) comes
largely from architectural staff in the Toronto and Montreal head offices.
All of the banks maintain that they design each bank individually to
meet local conditions, and all claim sensitivity to local needs. Most have
favourite design characteristics, however, that often get in the way.
The Toronto Dominion Bank works to achieve a strong roof-line for
recognition and as a background for signs; the Bank of Montreal avoids
large expanses of glass because openness might project an image of
instability, and the Royal Bank likes brick for its maintenance values.
Most banks say that they no longer use standardized designs; only the
Bank of Nova Scotia admits to having plans available on the shelf, although with variations and different materials for each part of the
country. Nevertheless, although banks frequently operate from branches
built for them by private developers, the latter are often big-city firms

The Toronto Dominion Bank in Nelson, British Columbia, is housed in a building quite unsympathetic to its neighbours. The curvilinear geometry and low massing are inappropriate when seen in the context of the street.

that have little sensitivity to the towns in which they work, and the results have included many disasters.

Decisions on banking needs are made by regional managers, who check on size and facilities in relation to size and location of the existing building. If additional space is needed, the first option is to expand on to the parking lot at the rear, if there is one. Although this is the easiest and most unobtrusive approach, local parking requirements often prohibit it. The next choices are usually an empty adjacent site or the building next door. Construction in stages thus permits the bank to avoid the need for temporary relocation. If no adjacent property is available, the bank will build an entirely new branch on an appropriate site nearby. This has increasingly been the rule. Although bank designers maintain that they work in harmony with local architectural conditions, a walk down Main Street often gives the contrary impression. New buildings bearing all the signs of the banks (and trust companies, caisses, and credit unions) often seem to have been designed with little sympathy for the existing street. For the most part architects have difficulty designing an infill building, one that takes the existing streetscape as its principal criterion for design. They seem more intent on creating a big statement, on designing a building that will contrast with its environment rather than complement it.

Banks have always produced strong architectural statements, so the current situation is nothing new. What has been lost is the architects' ability to make this statement in a way that fits a new building into the context of its surroundings. The banks' record of renovating existing buildings has not been much better. Whether because of the need to retain parking lots, the unavailability of adjacent land, or the corporations' desire to update their images with new buildings, renovation and expansion have not occurred as often as might be expected. The banks' planners maintain that certain features of older banks are inappropriate to modern use. Front steps (typical of classical 'temple' banks), for instance, hinder access by disabled and elderly customers. Interior columns interfere with standard counter design. Second storeys cause potential security risks. Damp basements provide poor staff facilities. Real as these situations may be, they are to some extent simply used as excuses to demolish older buildings. Placed in the hands of a good architect, such problems could be redefined as opportunities to achieve designs that were better than run-of-the-mill.

The future may see designers and property managers showing greater sensitivity and banks again becoming strong and sympathetic cornerstones of Main Street. Certainly things have moderated in the past fifteen years. The banks are still developing new branches, but they show a willingness to pay somewhat more attention to local conditions and, in a few cases, to existing buildings. The causes are many, including the heritage movement, economic restraints, and a growing respect for individuality. As competition resurfaces, due to competition from the trust companies, credit unions, and caisses, rivalry may well become a design factor again. For all that, the increasing automation of banking services may soon reshape the bank into a set of instant-teller machines along the sidewalk or in a parking lot.

Public Buildings

If historically the bank was one eye-catching presence on Main Street, another was certainly the post office. Fifty years ago, a small-town rendezvous – 'I'll meet you at the post office' – would have been easy for a stranger. The post office, probably built of stone, with a prominent and welcoming doorway and capped by a clock tower, had a strong architectural presence. Today that same meeting would not be so easy to arrange. The post office might well be a low, one-storey building a block or two off Main Street, anonymous in appearance and distinguished only by the red, white, and blue-banded sign stating the town's name and postal code.

The initial eagerness to provide symbols for a maturing society has given way to concerns for efficiency, and little effort has been made to merge the two. The federal Department of Public Works was reorganized in 1953 to streamline procedures. Decisions – and, by extension, designs – began to be made by committees rather than individuals. In the words of Public Works official historian Douglas Owram, a federal department which needed a new building 'got what it needed and the committee ensured – or did its best to ensure – that it did not get an unnecessarily expensive or elaborate building.' He comments: 'It was not the highly personalized approach of earlier years, but it was efficient.'

This shift in approach coincided with new design trends. The international style of architecture was quickly adopted by Public Works, especially after the department's reorganization under the new minister, Robert Winters. Chief architect E.A. Gardner undertook a renewed campaign of erecting federal buildings. Hard rectilinear structures with brick walls, flat roofs, and large expanses of windows arose everywhere. Their modern lines often proved incompatible with the traditional architecture of small communities. Few respected local materials or building sizes and shapes, and thus the buildings failed to fit comfortably into their environments. In the 1960s yet another change occurred. Post offices, now separated from other government functions, became small, usually brick boxes built to standard designs and often located on less-expensive land away from the town centre. The federal building ceased to be a landmark.

In the past two decades, an even more rigid system has governed the establishment of new post offices. In many respects it is typical of how large national organizations, public or private, operate within smaller centres. The decision to rebuild, relocate, or open a new post-office branch is made by a regional division of Canada Post through market surveys. The area and population to be served will determine the size of the facility to be built, which in turn will determine the exact plan of the new building. For smaller towns, Public Works builds what it calls its s2 series of post offices. These are five off-the-shelf designs, now more than twenty years old, that are based on various floor areas from 748 gross square feet (SP 1) to 3,136 gross square feet (SP 5). The SP does not stand for small post office; it stands for Standard Plan. The Department of Public Works is also responsible for site selection. Public Works analyses the requirements and offers Canada Post a selection of available sites. Once chosen, the land is purchased through the Department of Public Works, and the branch post office built.

The criteria underlying site selection are set out in a 1973 manual titled *Small Town Post Office Development: Town Planning Aspects*. Four series of criteria are described. According to the first three – physical, technical-legal, and economic criteria – the land should be available and not prohibitively expensive and should be suitable for construction, with adequate drainage and practical topography. Beyond these basic factors are social and environmental criteria. In theory an assessment in terms of these conditions would benefit Main Street:

The site should relate to, and if possible, enhance existing community features or functions. In this way it should contribute to rather than detract from the community it serves. Ideally it should be located near other public or commercial uses ... It should relate to surrounding architectural and aesthetic conditions ...
The site should have high visibility to promote the federal presence in the community.

Many will recognize that recent post-office locations do not seem to meet these criteria and that the post office is moving off Main Street. The trend is away from the older business districts, out of supposedly inefficient, oversized, and costly facilities and into compact locations away from the centre of town, with generous parking and access – or, even more radically, into the modern-age surrogate Main Street: the shopping centre. These moves have been brought about by a series of complex

The massive towered city hall in Nelson, British Columbia, built in 1902 as a post office. Federal offices are now housed in the Gray building next door, a representative exercise in the design principles of the modern movement.

The post office in St-Ours, Quebec, built in 1940, belongs to the last generation of traditionally styled federal buildings.

economic and social factors and not by a conscious effort to forsake federal architectural heritage.

Now that Canada Post has become a crown corporation, it will be independent of Public Works operations and will assume all of its own real-estate and property functions. While it is within the broad policy guidelines (established in 1979 by the Treasury Board) for the Department of Public Works to take into account social, economic, and environmental factors in real-property management (by taking into account local, regional, and provincial development plans and strategies; extent of local acceptance; and compatibility with the local neighbourhood in terms of land-use possibilities, aesthetics, and neighbourhood characteristics), a crown corporation administering the postal service is not governed by such guidelines. To date Canada Post has indicated that it does not feel bound to respect the limits of historical preservation or town planning in its future property-management decisions.

It is the architectural legacy of older federal buildings that will form the continuing battleground between Canada Post – which will not underwrite the costs of preserving heritage – and local pressures to retain as many of those buildings as possible. While the postal service may be housed in the most important building in town, Canada Post denies that it has the mandate to increase the costs of its service through building rehabilitation. Currently the corporation is undertaking an assessment of the costs and benefits of its existing property inventory. It is to be hoped that the corporation will realize the intangible benefits of being associated with its older buildings and with Main Street. There are signs that it may be happy to sell off some of its buildings to local groups for other needs.

Other public-sector buildings have drifted away from Main Street. The government-operated liquor store, a peculiarly Canadian institution reflecting the pervasive influence of the temperance movement (drink was a vice, and its sale thus required control boards), was at one time a Main Street component. Indeed, in some towns, such as Yellowknife, it was almost the only significant landmark around. The government-run liquor store has traditionally been run as a store-front operation in older buildings, often leasing space from a private landlord. Now, as most provincial liquor-control boards change from counter service to self-service – perhaps a sign that the stigma is disappearing – they are finding that they require larger stores with wider aisles. Consequently, many older liquor stores have had to be abandoned and replaced. They have often moved to large sites, away from the centre of town, on lots big enough that tractor-trailer trucks can manoeuvre easily and customers can park their cars.

Finally, other public buildings not in the retail business have changed

In the 1960s the Department of Public Works introduced its Standard Plan post office for small towns. All lack the dignity of their predecessors. Efficiency dictates form, and location as well: these buildings were invariably sited away from the downtown core to avoid higher real-estate costs and vehicle congestion. In Sheho, Saskatchewan, a small Standard Plan is fittingly parked beside a Saskatchewan Telephone exchange, housed in a trailer.

sites in their communities. The town hall, historically home for police department, fire station, and sometimes market hall, has outgrown the nineteenth-century structure. Towns have their own planning departments, assessment and rates offices, and sundry other separate facilities. In some communities, there is now very little public presence on Main Street. In Oakville, Ontario, for example, the old copper-roofed post office lies empty on Main Street, made redundant by a larger federal building constructed a block north in the 1950s. City hall is nowhere in sight. It moved several miles north into a new complex housing courts and other public-service facilities for an enlarged regional district. Like so many commercial institutions, our public institutions have developed according to interests and forces that are independent of any traditional sense of community, and this has meant an ever-diminishing role for Main Street during the post-war years.

Part Two

Sheathing older buildings in new skins has been a misguided approach to the revitalization of downtowns.

JACQUES DALIBARD

The Historical Context

One of the earliest efforts to revitalize a Main Street was undertaken in 1955 on Magdalen Street in the English cathedral town of Norwich. In many ways Magdalen Street was quite ordinary: it featured the kinds of chain stores, local shops, banks, hotels, and pubs which can be found in shopping thoroughfares throughout Britain. It was typical in another way, too: many of its buildings were examples of fine nineteenth-century commercial and institutional architecture that had become run down.

There were many reasons for this dilapidation. During the Depression of the 1930s, upkeep money had been in short supply. The Second World War had similarly drained manpower and resources away from the home front. When attention reverted to the built environment in the early fifties, a new set of problems surfaced: some buildings had been defaced by grime; others had been torn down; yet others had been overshadowed by unsympathetic additions and infill. Added to all of these problems was a downtown business attitude which could only charitably be described as lethargic. For a long time, downtown shopping areas such as Magdalen Street had been the only game in town. Without competition, complacency had set in and with it an undeniable seediness. By the early 1960s another, quite different problem was looming: the first regional malls were being planned, a phenomenon which would soon attract great numbers of shoppers and institutions away from the centre of the community, thereby hastening its further decline.

The deterioration of streets like Magdalen forced the British Civic Trust, a national preservation charity, to modify its conception of the targets at which preservation efforts should be directed. Previously, whenever people had talked about the built environment and the need to preserve it, thoughts had inevitably turned to great buildings. Heritage was thought of in terms of cathedrals, palaces, castles – the extraordinary features of the built environment. Turning attention to the ordinary buildings on Main Street was a revolutionary new way for heritage preservationists to look at their surroundings.

The Civic Trust wondered whether the appearance of the commercial areas in Norwich could be improved without major alterations or expense. Magdalen Street was chosen as a suitable case for experimentation because it was so typical and reflected so much that was then wrong with traditional shopping areas. The make-over of Magdalen Street was an energetic undertaking. The Civic Trust made certain that the project involved as many people as possible. Local shopkeepers were asked to participate (and eighty-two of eighty-four agreed), and so were civic leaders, corporate leaders, the fire department, and the bus company, the police, the media, and local preservation groups. Within a year of the project's launch, sixty-six properties were repainted in co-ordinated colours; twenty-two unsightly billboards were removed; seventeen signboards were redesigned; six lamp standards were replaced; a church was floodlit; overhead wiring was buried; bus shelters were made more attractive; and an empty parking lot was turned into a little city park. When the face-lifting was complete, most observers agreed that the Trust's first, tentative attempt to prettify a Main Street was a success.

This initial success encouraged imitation. In the following year, the Civic Trust undertook a tougher challenge in the Potteries town of Burslem. When a part of that town's uncompromisingly grimy main street was also transformed into an attractive shopping area, the Civic Trust knew that it had formulated a scheme of importance. In the following years more than four hundred similar projects were undertaken throughout Britain. By the mid 1960s the scheme had crossed the Atlantic. In the United States, where similar downtown problems were being experienced, the scheme became known as 'beautification.' In Canada it became known as the Norwich Plan.

The Norwich Union Life Insurance Society's plan for downtown restoration was undertaken first in the Ontario communities of Oakville and Niagara Falls. The scheme was voluntary, with each merchant paying the cost of refurbishing his premises and contributing by special assessment to the costs of tree planting, flower baskets, flags, and other street improvements. The Norwich Union promoted the plan widely. It distributed seventy thousand copies of a booklet and made a film on the Niagara Falls experience. More than two hundred towns and cities, mostly in Ontario, Nova Scotia, and British Columbia, adopted the plan.

Another Norwich-like plan was undertaken in Alberta. Called Main Street Alberta, it was a project of the Calgary-based Devonian Group of charitable foundations. Between 1973 and 1980, the Devonian Group entered into contracts with 161 communities in Alberta and a further 12 in British Columbia. This fifteen-million-dollar project encouraged a host of changes. These included new street furniture and planters, pocket parks, and the face-lifting of some buildings.

For all of this, however, beautification projects, from the Magdalen Street experiment to the Main Street Alberta project, were destined to be disappointing. With the advantage of hindsight it is easy to point out that in a fundamental way the beautification experiment simply did not work. The high hopes that were held out for it proved in time to be anchored by unsteady principles. From the beginning, prettification was based on the premise that all that was needed to resuscitate a central shopping core was a cosmetic fix-up. The Civic Trust's early literature unblushingly praises the superficial: its pamphlets boast that paint was the number-one expense; that the scheme was only surface deep; that the idea was to find ways to lay a gloss over the ugliness. Because it operated in this way, because it underestimated the complexity of a community, the scheme was doomed to failure. In Alberta the prettification scheme introduced paving materials, furniture, and landscaping that were frequently inappropriate to the character of the Alberta streetscape; new aluminum siding defaced many buildings; key buildings were demolished to make way for unneeded parks. Worse, the underlying problems facing many downtown districts were not addressed. As the Civic Trust itself has admitted in recent years, the early beautification schemes were successful only until the paint began to fade. Soon, the underlying problems which increasingly threatened Main Street proved too powerful to be held off by skin-deep solutions – by solutions that ignored a town's essential character.

By the mid-seventies the failures of the Norwich approach were recognized in Britain and the United States. Steps were taken, consequently, to address the problems of centre-town decay. In England, under the Civic Trust's Michael Middleton, the paint tins were downplayed and sophisticated schemes were developed to bring life back into centre-town. The result was improved downtowns in such places as Halifax, Glasgow, and Chester. In the United States, meanwhile, under Mary Means of the National Trust for Historic Preservation, three small midwest communities – Hot Springs, South Dakota; Madison, Indiana;

and Galesburg, Illinois – were made pilot projects for the first American Main Street project. In these towns, the idea was no longer merely to prettify the centre area but to get at the root problems of its decline. With the backing of local politicians, preservationists, and, most importantly, local merchants, plans were launched to attract and keep shoppers downtown. The approach was twofold: adopt the highly effective management techniques that the competition, the modern shopping centre, was using; and, at the same time, promote assets (such as delightful downtown architecture) that were unavailable to the new shopping centres. Encouraged by the preliminary findings in these communities, the National Trust created a National Main Street Center in Washington, DC, and sponsored a competition among the states for participation in a co-operative program. Almost all the communities experienced building rehabilitation, vacancy reduction, increased tourism, renewed community pride in local heritage – and a general downtown economic revitalization.

When I became the executive director of the Heritage Canada Foundation in 1978, I quickly turned my attention to the work of our Main Street colleagues abroad. As I saw it, the experiments that they were conducting were very close to what Canadian preservation should be all about. I knew, however, that if we launched a Main Street program of our own, it would mean a major shift in the foundation's direction.

The Heritage Canada Foundation had been launched in 1973 thanks to a twelve-million-dollar federal government endowment. Before that time the government had already distinguished itself in building preservation: forty-eight national historic sites were protected by a section of the Indian and Northern Affairs Department (now Parks Canada). But since the centennial year a widespread call had arisen for an agency that would help to preserve worthwhile buildings that were yet not historic sites. The Heritage Canada Foundation was set up as an independent national charity to push for the preservation of such buildings.

When the foundation was launched, however, there was still a tendency to think of heritage building in a very restricted way. A heritage building was one of a handful of special structures in the community: the post office, the town hall, the church, the local mansion. My view encompassed much more than that. To me, Canada's built heritage meant nothing less than that great mass of buildings, both special and vernacular, that makes us look the way we do. From a fishing village in Nova Scotia to a wheat town in Saskatchewan, it is the sum of our entire building, our entire man-made environment which gives us our special character.

Even a cursory look at our communities tells us that the buildings which give those communities their special character are concentrated in the oldest parts of town – the traditional downtown. I therefore came to the conclusion that preservation groups abroad had come to: that the best way to save the built environment was to concentrate not on saving one building here and one building there but instead on saving nothing less than the traditional heart of Main Street Canada. And thus was launched the Heritage Canada Foundation's Main Street program.

The first step, I knew, was for the foundation to go out into the field and learn as much as we could about a number of key issues. What exactly is a Main Street? Is it a single street? Is it a district? Who makes up Main Street? How does it work? What are its parts? What are its functions? Why has it deteriorated? What can be done to bring it back to life?

To learn all we could in a brief time, the foundation did two things. First, we chose, from the many applications that came in, seven communities from across the country. These were towns and cities which varied in topography, region, size, age, and problems. But all of them had downtowns that were full of splendid but endangered buildings. Next, we invented a new profession. We developed the idea of Main Street co-ordinators. A co-ordinator, paid by the foundation, lived in a demonstration community for three years. There he operated in some ways like a shopping-mall manager. Whereas in most downtown communities each merchant had been accustomed to going his own way, in a shopping centre there would be a manager who worked as a unifying force, showing merchants ways in which their combined efforts could yield greater results. A Main Street co-ordinator's function was to live in the community, learn how it worked, suggest solutions to problems, bring together the players needed to make Main Street live again.

The information gleaned from the first phase of the Main Street experiment is the subject of this book. What we learned is in these pages. In phase two, this information will be passed on to co-ordinators and managers in hundreds of towns and cities across the country. If the principles we have learned stand up, then we will, in the next decade, remake the face of Canada, returning to Main Street the life it both needs and enriches.

Downtown amenities: a little something for everyone in Moose Jaw,
Saskatchewan, circa 1912

JOHN STEWART

Breathing Life back into Downtown

Not everybody sat back and watched as the crisis on Main Street intensified. Some concerned individuals and communities have attempted to put new life into their local main streets. Sporadic, unorganized, sometimes even harmful at first, the efforts have recently become more widespread, co-ordinated, and constructive. Some of these were clearly local in their conception, implemented in a rather ad hoc fashion, and have had a variety of interesting consequences. Also at a local level, some schemes stressing the need for local decision-making found backing among private foundations. A second wave of change has come about as a result of provincial revitalization programs geared to improvements in appearance or profitability. In so far as each province has tailored programs to its own perception of problem and need, the consequent injection of energy and capital has varied across the country. A third approach has been launched by the Heritage Canada Foundation, with its small-town Main Street program. Communities of different sizes and characters and from different regions across the country have been chosen as demonstration projects for 'revitalization through preservation.'

Local Changes

Some towns seeking a renewed or better-defined community image have selected a national or period theme, and property owners have been asked to alter their buildings to conform to the local theme. This tendency has been strongest in British Columbia, where Kimberley has been transformed into a Bavarian village, Osoyoos has become pseudo-

Spanish in character, Grand Forks may go Doukhobor, and White Rock is Mediterranean. This theme treatment is usually little more than a fantasy and has little to do with rehabilitation or restoration; nevertheless, the approach can have its charms when carried off with flair. Kimberley's metamorphosis is perhaps the best, because the Alpine theme is appropriate to the town's developing fame as a ski centre. The municipality has encouraged the creation of half-timbered façades and the use of Gothic lettering and has drawn even more pedestrians downtown by developing a German-style *platz* on its Main Street. Osoyoos, at the southern end of the Okanagan Valley, similarly has many attributes that make its adopted Spanish motif successful. The increasing number of Portuguese families in the vicinity (representing a significant portion of the work force of the local orchard industry) and the region's dry, hot climate suggest a Mediterranean atmosphere. Whitewashed stucco walls and Spanish tile roofs, whether on the town hall, fire station, hardware store, or bank building, do not look out of place, perhaps because they echo Californian styles long popular in the province.

Farther east the town of Battleford, Saskatchewan, has gone 'Wild West frontier.' Battleford is a town of two thousand, close to the prosperous regional centre of North Battleford (population thirteen thousand). In the early 1970s a group of Battleford citizens led by Town Clerk Eileen Barry decided to do something to spruce up their Main Street, Twenty-second Street West. Its stores were being neglected by local shoppers and passed by quickly by tourists on their way to Battleford National Historic Park. A planning study prepared in 1974 by Saskatoon's Consultant Group Limited concluded that the town could re-establish commercial vigour with economic and physical changes that would include fixing up the store-fronts along Main Street and 'emphasizing the strong historical heritage of the town.' It recommended that some buildings receive a 'minor face-lift' and others the 'construction of an historical façade.' Work began around 1976, with property owners paying for the work on their buildings. Battleford suddenly went neo-frontier. The street that emerged is lined with rustic cedar-faced buildings against which lean porches and posts. Many were designed by David Hiley, a member of the original consultant team. The graphics continue the Wild West theme. The Bank of Montreal, the only chartered bank in town, moved from a handsome but decidedly unfashionable 1912 block into a small new cedar-faced strip mall, and the credit union from North Battleford built a local branch in cedar.

The town may have gained its 'historical façades,' but the history looks back to the American cinema and not to Saskatchewan. The new frontier bears little resemblance to the true character of the town as it was originally built in the first decade of the century. The observer is left asking whether Battleford was not carried away by its enthusiasm and whether all of this was a good thing. Certainly the townsfolk are proud of what has happened, and business does seem to have taken an upswing. Lyle Trost, manager of the Battleford Food Fair, attributes a 50 per cent increase in grocery sales over three years to the new store-fronts. The town now has a sense of identity and of place, even if the old has been destroyed by trying to look older.

Face-lifting campaigns can, however, have positive results. We might look at Corning, New York, where the Market Street Restoration Agency's Norman Mintz directed a program to improve the local Market Street. Too often, face-lifting has meant denuding the building – exposing brick and stripping wood – without replacing anything. What is more constructive is to improve renovated store-fronts with a rational de-sign effort, however simple it may be. One option is the actual restora-tion of the original materials, finishes, and forms. This may, however, be too expensive or may look too old-fashioned to satisfy merchandising needs. A second and equally valid option is rehabilitation. New materials may be used in a way that respects the composition and the lines of the original front. Aluminum and steel can be perfectly valid substitutes for wood when designed in a sensitive and sympathetic manner.

Unlike restoration, in which a building is returned to the state in which it existed at a particular date, rehabilitation, writes Mintz, in *A Practical Guide to Storefront Rehabilitation* (1977), 'should be considered a contemporary solution which respects the architectural integrity of the entire building front.' Rehabilitation focuses on 'retaining those ele-ments that enhance the building and removing those – such as poorly designed and conflicting signs and unattractive "false" fronts – that de-tract [from] or conceal it … The original proportions, lines and textures of the building should be respected. Contemporary materials used in the rehabilitation should be compatible with older existing materials.'

Mintz showed that Corning's store-fronts could sometimes be im-proved for as little as $250 – for scraping off old paint and applying an appropriate new colour. Other buildings cost up to a few thousand dollars. But in each case he and his design staff helped property owners to find the way to reveal the integral features of the building, not simply to make the store-front look quaint or cute by adding period motifs or other gimmicks.

This understated approach to design is gradually becoming recog-nized as the best – often, as well, as the least expensive. The simple route also works well with planting, street furniture, paving, and other improvements to public areas. Introducing new materials may conflict with the traditional character of Main Street. The key is to work with existing features.

Provincial Rehabilitation Programs

The various independent experiments with Main Street rehabilitation projects have demonstrated their value in improving both businesses and appearances. They have also shown that Main Street needs help. In the last few years several provincial governments have tried to meet that need by instituting Main Street and revitalization programs which give assistance to municipalities and merchants hoping to improve the commercial viability of their downtown cores. Most programs offer some combination of grants, loans, design and technical assistance, and business-development aid. Many are linked with the concept of creating a 'business-improvement' area managed by local property owners and storekeepers.

These programs improve upon the principle of the face-lifting campaign by offering a more comprehensive revitalization package, with realistic options for financing. It is too soon to judge their results, but in many cases the programs do seem to help business. In other instances the schemes are threatening to redevelop town centres somewhat overenthusiastically and without proper regard for the true character of Main Street. And in almost every case, assistance for beautification, building rehabilitation, and business revitalization is fragmented rather than co-ordinated.

Generally speaking, three departments of provincial governments have an interest in Main Street. Departments or ministries related to municipal affairs (or housing) focus on planning issues, including beautification, land use, the provision of services, and new development. Departments that administer heritage legislation (usually cultural affairs) have an interest in the protection of buildings and areas of architectural or historical significance. Departments of commercial or industrial affairs aim to help businesses with marketing and other technical assistance. While many of the initiatives are effective, there has been little co-operation among the three spheres of interest (although things have improved in the last several years).

Ontario was the first province to address itself to the issue of Main Street decay in both large and small centres. It in turn owes something to the federal government's former Neighbourhood Improvement Program. NIP subsidized street improvements and services in specially designated areas. Administered by Canada Mortgage and Housing Corporation, it emphasized residential areas and aimed to improve the

Rosberg's department store in Niagara Falls, Ontario, before (top) and after the application of the skin-deep solutions of the Norwich Plan to problems of downtown revitalization

A Devonian Group 'pocket park' in Fort Macleod, Alberta, infrequently used and until recently rarely maintained

housing situation, whereas the provinces' programs are directed at commercial revitalization. Under the Ontario Ministry of Municipal Affairs
and Housing, programs of aid to municipalities were established. Each
related to a particular scale of urban community, and all shared a
common goal – the physical and commercial rejuvenation of downtown
shopping districts through grants to established joint committees drawn
from merchants' groups and the community at large. Extremely successful, these programs accomplished all they were intended to do and have
been phased out. Their approaches are now used in the Community
Area Improvement Program (CAIP), begun in 1984. This is a four-year
program but with far more limited funds, under the current phase of
fiscal restraint, than had been available earlier. CAIP had a 1983–4 budget
of six million dollars, and twenty-two communities took advantage of
these funds. The maximum provincial contribution is five hundred thousand dollars, matched by the municipality. A maximum one-third could
be a grant, with the other two-thirds a loan to be repaid over ten years at
half the provincial borrowing rate.

Two of the most successful of the earlier programs, now phased out,
were the Ontario Main Street and the Ontario Downtown Revitalization
programs. The Ontario Main Street Revitalization Program, for towns of
35,000 or less, helped some fifty-five communities. The Ontario Downtown Revitalization Program was directed at communities of up to
125,000 and offered larger amounts for major improvements (including
downtown malls). The program offered front-end funding to municipalities for beautification: litter baskets, street lighting, signage, parking
facilities, and so on. Property could be acquired by the municipality
for downtown improvement; this usually involved land for parking but
also included buildings acquired in order to conserve them. The provincial loan was to a maximum of $150,000 and provincial recovery of 110
per cent over a ten-year period. The money was not to be used for ongoing maintenance, planning, or marketing, and no funding was available for privately owned property. A business-improvement area (BIA),
managed by local merchants, had to be set up under the provisions of
the Ontario Municipal Act. The BIA management committee was required
to allow at least 50 per cent of its budget for the repayment of the loan.

The Ontario Downtown and Main Street Revitalization programs
were intended to assist downtowns to compete with suburban and
regional shopping malls. In several cases communities used these funds
to develop new downtown shopping centres. Cornwall Square is one
example. The mall unfortunately turns its back on Cornwall's historic
Pitt Street and may hurt established stores more than it helps them.
The province cannot impose rigid guidelines, however; in its ongoing

Osoyoos, British Columbia, has gone Spanish. The textures of the village hall, resplendent in its stucco walls and tile roof, have been encouraged everywhere in town.

programs it cannot intervene in what have to be municipal decisions. The Community Renewal Branch of the ministry does prepare information kits under PRIDE (Programs for Renewal, Improvement, and Development) and clearly helps to energize local BIAS with a range of catalogues on what might be possible. Two other provincial initiatives can affect Ontario main streets. The Ministry of Industry and Tourism offers two education programs for small-business development, and the Ministry of Culture and Recreation provides the means for designating and funding heritage-conservation districts.

The Saskatchewan Main Street Development Program was administered jointly by the provincial Department of Municipal Affairs (which made Business Improvement District grants directly to the business community for improvements to public property) and the Department of Industry and Commerce (which made grants to private business persons for store-front improvements). Funding for these grants was exhausted in 1983. The objective of the program was to 'secure the economic base of rural Saskatchewan communities by assisting towns and their business people to improve their downtown areas.' The grants amounted to cash reimbursements for up to 50 per cent of store-front improvements, to a maximum of five hundred dollars per business. Only communities of six thousand or less were eligible – and at least 75 per cent of eligible businesses in a formally designated business-improvement district had to agree to carry out renovations 'based on a commonly agreed-upon scheme.'

Unlike Ontario, the Saskatchewan government took a direct, hands-on approach to technical and design assistance. The guide to self-help provided to municipalities makes many design-improvement suggestions, among them the 'removal of old untidy signs or other features, including entire old façades if necessary.' A large and profusely illustrated Saskatchewan Main Street Design Catalogue, prepared by two architecture students for the provincial Department of Industry and Commerce, offers some good advice. It shows how a masonry building can be restored to its former grace by the removal of a modern cornice and the addition of canopies, and how visual peace can be bestowed on a building, marred by unsightly new siding, when the siding is removed and the bricks revealed. It advises that, in a town of frame buildings, often no changes are required on the structures themselves, and elsewhere only the elimination of previous attempts at decoration, to create new clean lines. The Design Catalogue freely – and at times, too enthusiastically – recommends landscaping features such as paving blocks, trees, plants, and benches to serve as unifying elements.

The first Saskatchewan Main Street program was completed in the historic town of Battleford, where guidelines were established to give buildings the Wild West look described above. After the town had begun its pioneering, government funds helped to pay for street paving, a new median strip, cement sidewalks (boardwalks were considered but rejected as being dangerous for high heels), a storm sewer, and new streetlights (which merchants admit have been scaled much too tall for the one-storey structures). The government program lauds Battleford for being its pilot project.

The Nova Scotia Main Street Program began experimentally in 1978 as an attempt to clean up the towns that were the gateways into the province: Amherst, Digby, Yarmouth, and North Sydney. Although considerable government resources were being expended to promote the province as a tourist destination, first impressions were not always in accord with the glossy magazine advertisements. The gateway program quickly spread, and most communities have now benefited in one form or another. The Department of Development co-ordinates its direction of the program with the Department of Municipal Affairs. The scheme provides a variety of funding levels for downtown refurbishment. This ranges from 100 per cent assistance for the labour costs of public works in downtown areas (such as roadwork, landscaping, and the burying of services) to 30 per cent of the costs of façade improvements to private businesses (to a maximum of $2,500 per business).

Responsibility for the execution of the work is placed on a local business-improvement-district committee. A business-improvement district (BID) may be established in a community of any size, although there are funding limits of $75,000 for public-works labour costs in towns, villages, and unincorporated communities. Funds are also available on a shared basis for long-term planning and for architectural and engineering studies. Towns may also form a downtown-development corporation as an ongoing concern representing business interests and funded by subscription from the business community. Legislation passed in 1981 now enables the formation of a business-improvement-district commission, which is empowered to levy special taxes.

The program offers guidance in such matters as store-front design and signage and will share the costs of design studies. Most Nova Scotia communities are less than three thousand people in size and cannot be expected to have sophisticated design and planning skills close at hand. The program offers guidelines that indicate a clear range of procedures through which to gain support for communities, and seems willing to entertain local initiatives. John Thorpe, the program's co-ordinator, notes that many Nova Scotia towns were built in a hurry, often after devastating fires. As a result numerous communities do not

Store-fronts along Twenty-second Street West in Battleford, Saskatchewan, acquired cedar false fronts, porches, and fences as part of a plan to promote the town's 'strong historical heritage.'

A postcard of Battleford in 1908. The false fronts are there, but nowhere are there porches or stained rustic façades, historical references that, it appears, look back to Hollywood rather than to the Saskatchewan frontier.

Cornwall Square and its parking garage in downtown Cornwall, Ontario, turn their backs on historic Pitt Street. This project was financed by the Ontario Downtown Revitalization Program, which cannot intervene in municipal decisions concerning how the funds will be used.

have many attractive buildings downtown. For this reason the thrust of
the program is to get owners to upgrade – with the aid of planned
design guidelines – rather than to go back to origins.

One feels in Nova Scotia that part of this emphasis on upgrading
reflects a sense of urgency concerning the need to respond to shopping
centres; these have dramatically changed retailing habits in the province in the last decade. Bridgewater, for example, a town of six thousand
people on the south shore, has been severely affected by the proximity
of three shopping malls. The downtown had been reduced to convenience stores, and there was only an institutional shell remaining. The
efforts of the Main Street program have helped to turn around the town
in two years. One block now has a distinct village atmosphere; there are
new sidewalks composed of local aggregate; the town hall will stay
put rather than be rebuilt elsewhere in the community; and an old bank
has been turned into a public library. Inner-block parking discreetly
placed behind buildings helps to make the town attractive.

Across the province, many towns now have a dramatically new
visual appearance. This seems a little sad, particularly if there is now an
overwhelming modernity that masks a community's historic charm.
Certainly the columns of brand-new lamp standards, bricked sidewalks,
and cleaned-up store-fronts make Wolfville different from what it was
a few years ago. Importantly, it was local political initiative that led to
this solution, not some external government fiat, and the result has
been a reinvigorated commercial area. In the face of the threat from the
malls Nova Scotia has reason to be optimistic. As Carol Conrad, the
province's Main Street program administrator, comments: 'We have begun to develop the image, to get people curious, create a more pedestrian
scale; through this people realize, bit by bit, that they can get what
they want on Victoria Street rather than out at the mall.'

In British Columbia, the Ministry of Municipal Affairs announced its
Downtown Revitalization Program in 1980. This scheme offers a start-
up grant of $5,000 to any municipality or recognized group wanting to
undertake initial promotion and discussion of downtown improvement. A loan of up to $10,000 will assist with the costs of design advice.
If work proceeds, grants of up to 20 per cent, to a maximum of two
hundred dollars per metre, are available for façade improvements within
specified areas. No specific guidelines are given to explain what constitutes an improvement. Loans of up to $375,000 will help with as much
as 75 per cent of the costs of municipal improvements. Further un-
specified funding assistance is available through the designation of
special areas. This program was intended to have been co-ordinated
with the Heritage Area Revitalization Program administered by the

British Columbia Heritage Trust, but so far the two programs have
operated independently. The Ministry of Industry and Small Business
assists individual entrepreneurs independently of the Downtown Revitalization Program. Nelson has been the pilot project for these
schemes, and Vancouver Island communities such as Courtenay and
Campbell River have already seen dramatic changes to their main
streets.

Manitoba began its own Main Street program in 1982 under the
umbrella of the Ministry of Municipal Affairs. The impetus yet again was
the shopping-centre syndrome. Smaller communities were dying as
consumers travelled to malls to find a larger selection. According to Elsie
Forrest, whose Budget and Finance Section supervises the $1.5 million-
a-year program, people wanted 'somewhere to sit down and socialize in
a place that was nicer, so we decided to try to let them sit down and
socialize at home.' The province gives municipalities two-thirds of the
cost of new sidewalks, pocket parks, street furniture, and lighting.
Individual store owners can receive one-third of the costs, up to a total
of five hundred dollars, for face-lifts to their buildings. Not to be used
for structural change, the funds help with new signs, lighting, steps,
and painting. Applications are checked by the Cultural and Historical
Resources Ministry to ensure that no heritage structure is to be significantly altered. Erickson, a small (two-elevator) town near Riding
Mountain National Park, was the first community to participate in the
program, followed by Swan River and Flin Flon. Even small unincorporated district settlements such as Landmark have received funds.
Twelve municipalities are committed to the program at the moment, with
a further fifteen assembling their applications.

New Brunswick has a program in place on paper, but as yet there is no
groundswell of activity, and in few places does response to these
funds at a local level seem to have arisen. Moncton, suffering severely
from a downtown mall and five fringe malls, has a Main Street that is a
ghost of its former glory. While it has the will to improve, plans are still
being developed. Chatham, suffering from the closure of CFB Chatham
and various plywood mills, is also beginning to talk about revitalization
schemes; current plans see the waterfront as the major beneficiary.

The government of Quebec has recently established a Main Street
program, RéviCentre, which offers assistance to municipalities that
are experiencing downtown deterioration and the threat from regional
shopping centres. Advice in the areas of downtown image, publicity,
marketing, business conditions, building renovations, and physical
services is provided in publications that are issued by the provincial
Ministry of Municipal Affairs' program 'pour orienter le réaménagement

d'un centre-ville.' Aid comes in the form of technical and planning expertise as well as outright cash grants. The program applies to cities and towns of any size and is open to municipalities which have requested assistance. The provincial government has also enacted legislation which allows business-improvement areas – sociétés d'initiative et de développement des artères commerciales, or SIDACS – to permit communities to create a tax levy to fund economic revitalization. Neighbourhood shopping streets in the Montreal urban region also fall into this framework and may soon be undertaking initiatives in the Main Street direction.

Prince Edward Island offers no scheme of its own but uses federal funds intended for social and economic development to help with community improvements and building rehabilitation. 'Most of our own discretionary funding is tied to social services such as education and hospitals,' says Ron MacNeil, the Department of Community Affairs Municipal Relations adviser. 'Unless we get federal assistance, it is hard to do a Main Street-type program here on the Island.'

Newfoundland and Alberta offer no provincial programs for downtown revitalization. Alberta's downtowns have, however, been affected by the Devonian Group's Main Street Alberta program.

The Heritage Canada Foundation Approach

Since its formation in 1973, the Heritage Canada Foundation has been developing a broad base in its approach to the Canadian past. Some initiatives have been highly technical, such as the workshops and booklets on paint-stripping, wood treatments, and stone repair, all focusing on the stabilizing of structures. The desire to preserve the past for present and future generations has sometimes led to highly publicized campaigns geared to saving threatened structures; over time this impulse has been redirected towards efforts to develop a conservation consciousness that could make such last-minute rescues less and less necessary. In this context, the emerging concern over streetscapes, heritage districts, and heritage areas – beyond specific landmark structures – has revealed a need for activity on a broader scale and for exploring ways of marrying heritage preservation with contemporary economic needs.

As funds became available from various provincial and federal programs, the foundation attempted to define the possibilities and choices that lay before it. Was it possible to channel these resources, inculcate a sense of pride and change in a downtown group, and, through professional design advice, facilitate physical and economic change? In the

The Ontario Main Street Revitalization Program financed these amenities for pedestrians and street improvements on Princess Street in Kingston, Ontario.

Market Street, Corning, New York, 1981, and the results of a model campaign of practical and understated store-front rehabilitation

United States, the National Trust's Main Street scheme had shown that preservation and economic revitalization could go hand in hand rather than be in conflict. A set of manuals and workshops was spreading the word in the United States. Was this possible in Canada as well? In many ways the social fabric, histories, and economic realities were similar. Some critical differences in tax structures, government actions, and planning legislation meant that a different approach might have to be tailored for Canadian communities.

It is clear that there is – and long has been – more than one method of approaching revitalization. Some of the provincial programs are somewhat ambivalent towards heritage-preservation agendas. In their rush to implement capital improvements that modernize, many schemes sow the seeds of their own eventual demise. Many of these stitched-on improvements, if not done in close conjunction with individual merchants and owners, are fads. Like a puppy bought with enthusiasm but then neglected when the need for routine long-term care asserts itself, many schemes suffer from lack of foresight.

The Heritage Canada approach has not been to emphasize public improvements, which for many projects is their starting- and end-point. The foundation has sponsored a Main Street program aimed at instilling new life into Canadian downtowns. The goal is to combine preservation techniques with economic and social revitalization of a community's commercial centre through a gradual process of incremental change. The foundation further hopes that its activities will help to stimulate the labour-intensive renovation industry and therefore assist in creating jobs. The program shows Main Street merchants that preservation is good business and makes better sense for older commercial centres than other approaches to revitalization. By preservation, the foundation means capitalizing on a community's history and character without turning it into a theme village. Through efforts that strengthen Main Street's existing assets – including its architectural heritage and its commercial and social diversity – downtown can thrive once again. The ultimate goal is to improve the quality of life on Main Street. The program operates on the premise that the consistent advocacy and professional guidance of an on-site project co-ordinator will result in greater participation by individuals and will be far more cost-efficient than would the short-term reports of consultants. Of fundamental importance is that it requires only minimal infusions of public monies.

The key is community involvement and self-help. The Heritage Canada Foundation, in its pilot projects, sent project co-ordinators to live in project communities to work closely with local leaders. Each co-ordinator offered free assistance on all matters from design to advertising but left

top This mall, separated from downtown Bridgewater, Nova Scotia, by the La Have River, is one of three malls that have seriously damaged the retail health of the downtown.

bottom In spite of the malls, downtown Bridgewater has begun to reassert itself with the help of the province's Main Street program.

New lamps, paving bricks, and new façade materials in Wolfville, Nova Scotia, another beneficiary of the province's Main Street program

final decisions to the merchants themselves. The program co-ordinators did not go in and tell people what they should do. They helped them to recognize what in their buildings was worth preserving and enhancing. The same approach was taken with economic matters. The foundation developed these techniques after studying a number of existing programs. Models included Canada Mortgage and Housing Corporation's Neighbourhood Improvement Program, which placed a local project manager in an advocacy role, and the Civic Trust's design work in Norwich, England. Heritage Canada learned the most from the United States National Trust for Historic Preservation's Main Street project. That project's structuring of activities in pilot communities into four distinct components – including organization, downtown promotion, preservation, and economic restructuring – became a keystone of the Heritage Canada Foundation Main Street program.

Given the foundation's philosophy that it is better to show by example than to tell people what to do, the Main Street program first directed its attention to the attractive town of Perth, Ontario (population six thousand). The results since November 1981 have been rewarding. In a period of recession and tight money, new businesses have opened in Perth and a number of property owners have taken advantage of the free design service available through the project. The town has a whole new look to it. Over a two-year period the project in Perth generated fourteen dollars in private investments for every dollar spent in the community by the Heritage Canada Foundation. The town was also able to attract important federal and provincial grants to assist in the upgrading process.

Nelson, British Columbia (population ten thousand), was named the second pilot community in July 1981. A regional centre nestled in the scenic Kootenay Mountains, Nelson saw its central business district suffer a blow with the opening of the Chahko-Mika shopping mall close to downtown. Encouraged by strong provincial support and funding, extensive private renovations and public improvements were carried out over the three years of the Heritage Canada presence.

There are now seven communities that have been involved in pilot projects. By providing a variety of models, these communities have allowed the foundation to understand the problems and restrictions confronting independent businesses and property owners. The communities were selected from across Canada through a Main Street selection process. The applicants were evaluated in four categories: architectural character, economic capability, organizational commitment, and administrative ability. The communities reflected something of the

Gore Street, Perth, Ontario, in 1981, at the start of Heritage Canada's first Main Street demonstration project

country's geographic diversity, architectural types, and a range of economic, social, and population conditions.

Moose Jaw, Saskatchewan (population thirty-five thousand), and Fort Macleod, Alberta (population fifteen hundred), are both representative Prairie communities, albeit with different economic bases. Moose Jaw is an important divisional point on the Canadian Pacific Railway; it has some fine architecture along a dramatic Main Street that terminates at the station, but it had a retail structure that was threatened by new regional competition both in Regina and in its own backyard. Fort Macleod, originally a North-West Mounted Police fort, has strong historical traditions. But it was a small town that was watching its local rural population turn to Lethbridge and Calgary for its needs.

In Ontario, the city of Cambridge (population eighty thousand) was formed by amalgamation of the old communities of Galt, Preston, and Hespeler. Mill towns on the Grand River, they had watched their employment base erode as factories closed and new ones located elsewhere in the region. Aggressive downtowns in larger communities such as Waterloo and regional malls in a region of excellent roads meant that a dignified old Main Street in Galt was having trouble identifying its market area and was slipping as an attractive place to shop.

In the Maritimes, perhaps no area has felt the winds of change as much as the Annapolis Valley. Windsor (population ten thousand), an old shipping port in an area of strong agricultural heritage, and Bridgetown (population one thousand), some fifteen miles north of Digby, were two towns that had slipped in recent years. A significant portion of Windsor's population shopped and worked in Halifax. Many of Bridgetown's merchants apprehensively watched the construction of the approaching freeway, one that would take traffic off Granville Street but also away from their shops to larger malls up the valley.

The experience to date with Main Street communities indicates that the program's approach provides an excellent means for private and local investment and that the impact on small businesses is positive. The advantages of the Main Street approach are many: it requires little capital investment from businessmen; it is labour intensive; it creates employment using technical skills; and it can be phased in, as funds become available, without negative impact. It is the foundation's position that the survival – or, in some cases, the revival – of Main Street depends on an integrated approach. Physical improvements alone, even if enlightened in design and accomplished in execution, are hollow in substance and will wear out quickly unless accompanied by commercial revitalization. Conversely, economic strengthening without quality design guidance will more often than not bring about architectural changes that destroy the character of the area, wasting an important resource. Improvements to businesses and buildings must proceed together and must be guided by ongoing and effective management. Approached in this way, Main Street may once again and for many generations to come become the true focus of our nation's communities.

Twenty-fourth Street, Fort Macleod, Alberta, in 1982

Baker Street, Nelson, British Columbia, in 1983

Travellers Association parade on Main Street North in
Moose Jaw, Saskatchewan, 1982

Queen Street, Bridgetown, Nova Scotia, in 1984

Dickson Street, Cambridge, Ontario, in 1983

Downtown Windsor, Nova Scotia, in 1984

Part Three

A Business Improvement District meeting in Moose Jaw, Saskatchewan

JOHN EDWARDS

Organizing for Change

The first of Heritage Canada's pilot projects, in Perth, Ontario, got off to a poor start. The project, in fact, was nearly shelved before it began. Controversy had pitted the town and the foundation against each other, and the opposing postures reinforced some myths – the town wanting to modernize, the outside preservationists telling its citizens to keep something for their own good. At the centre of the disagreement was the decision to replace a bridge across the Tay River (part of the Tay–Rideau Canal system). This had nothing directly to do with the revitalization of Gore or Foster streets. The town saw the old, single-lane Drummond Street span as an impediment to effective traffic flow within and around the town. It believed that its demolition and replacement by a modern concrete bridge would help to solve that blockage and to attract new industry.

Heritage Canada, in contrast, saw this light, wooden-decked swing bridge as an historical gem and part of a landscape complex associated with the canal turning basin. Were the whole basin to be revitalized, as envisaged by Parks Canada, then the town had an important historical resource that would help tourism. To Heritage Canada, the bridge's restoration was essential. Indeed, the foundation threatened to withdraw its plans for Perth if the town did not replace the crumbling bridge with a replica – complete with working swing span and single-lane wooden deck.

In hindsight it is clear that Heritage Canada was playing what had been, till then, the traditional role of preservation agencies – the outside expert going into a community to offer advice on local preservation

This photograph was taken in 1940 from the water tower in Perth, Ontario. Until 1982 sizeable boats using the Rideau Canal system were able to dock in the centre of town. A modern concrete replacement of the Drummond Street bridge in the middleground now prevents the turning basin from being used in this manner.

problems. Here, such involvement was seen as interference. The damaging early publicity set the Perth Main Street project back at least a year. Perth residents misunderstood the intentions of 'these people telling us how to run our town.' When other contentious issues came up, such as the feasibility and desirability of a downtown mall, heated opinions concerning the Drummond Street bridge (built, eventually, in modern concrete) echoed around the debate.

A valuable lesson was learned from this disagreement, however. Outsiders should never cast themselves, or allow themselves to be cast, as experts telling 'misguided' citizens what is best for them. Advice and assistance may be appreciated and accepted – but only when a sense of trust has been established. A key part of that trust is feeling that the 'expert' cares for the place, understands its past, and respects its traditions. There are often good reasons why things have been done in certain ways. If it can be pointed out that such ways are less than efficient in the long run and that a different method could achieve better ends, support might be forthcoming. If there are ways other than demolition or radical refurbishing to make economic changes within an existing building, calm discussion might gain profitable results. It is better to talk long and often – in stores, on streets, in homes, and in council – than to preach through a megaphone on a passing truck.

In the other project communities, started after Perth and its bridge incident, the co-ordinators downplayed the image of the outside consultant. They appreciated, to be sure, the good publicity given to the news that Heritage Canada was coming to town. Often the opening of the Main Street office coincided with a media blitz and visits from Heritage Canada Foundation Chairman Pierre Berton and Executive Director Jacques Dalibard. Ideally the co-ordinators would then have preferred to have settled in quietly, learned about the town and its issues, and slowly begun to suggest some possibilities. The reality was often quite different. Quiet calm was disrupted by crisis or controversy that had been lurking near the surface. In Moose Jaw, the possibility of a major downtown mall large enough to compete with some of Regina's retailing activities would certainly have a major impact on the traditional Main Street merchants. A new regional mall in Lawrencetown, Nova Scotia, and an extension of the Annapolis Valley freeway around Bridgetown (both scheduled for completion by the mid 1980s) would have massive repercussions for the small enclave on Bridgetown's Queen and Granville streets. In Nelson, British Columbia, the Heritage Canada project began after a major schism had already occurred over plans to revitalize Baker Street. Merchant-led initiatives to upgrade the street and its buildings had been stalled while the City of Nelson and the regional-planning district had commissioned a $75,000 consultant study from a team of Vancouver architects and planners. While this plan accorded with many of the merchants' initial objectives, it had acquired 'big-city' associations, and any subsequent initiative would be gauged as being pro or anti this plan.

Such a threat, controversy, or crisis often helps to define options for a community and enables the co-ordinators to promote revitalization through preservation. Their approach, wherever possible, was not to offer a specific game-plan. They continued to work from inside and with the merchants rather than to impose a template for economic or design changes. In each project town the co-ordinators emphasized joining the community and becoming part of its life. In Windsor, Nova Scotia, Chris Pelham joined the Kinsmen; in Fort Macleod, Jim Mountain and his wife revived a theatrical troupe; and in Bridgetown, Peter Hyndman took up lawn bowling. These were rather obvious and visible attempts at joining the community. More pervasive were the benefits of simply setting up residence. In Perth, John Stewart sensed that he had begun to be recognized as having joined the community when he and his family attended the Rotary Club's Strawberry Social. After that, he was not just the Heritage Canada representative, in his office weekdays from nine to five, but one resident among the others, doing things in the town in the evenings and on weekends.

The potentially paralysing image of the outside consultant can be gradually shed as the co-ordinator gets on with the task – as a partner with the town – of trying to make the downtown work as the community's primary retail and public centre. There is no easy formula for this, of course. Even ten- or fifteen-year residents of some places can occasionally be regarded as newcomers. For a person clearly introduced as being on loan from the Heritage Canada Foundation for a limited period of time, the matter of fitting into small-town life can be an even greater problem. Further, there may be pitfalls in joining one but not other segments of a community. Even if the host group is the right one, there is the dilemma of being perceived as somewhat machiavellian. For the most part, however, the experience of the Heritage Canada co-ordinators has been highly positive.

Although joining a community has been an important early step, the co-ordinator must work overtime in order to understand how a town functions. Who are the leaders, both in the formal sense and also informally, exerting influence through the community's social network? Which groups are the most influential economically, socially, and culturally? Such individuals and groups, widely respected in the community, need to be brought on side, for their support can be a major boost

The proposed downtown mall in Moose Jaw, Saskatchewan, plans for which have now fortunately been shelved because of financial obstacles. The token heritage component involved maintaining one 'significant' house, shown in the right foreground.

CRESCENT PARK MALL PROPOSED DOWNTOWN REVITALIZATION BY R.& G. HOLDINGS LTD. MOOSE JAW, SASKATCHEWAN

The Main Street program in Nelson, British Columbia, began in the summer of 1981 with the restoration of the RHC Realty building on Baker Street.

The RHC building unveiled. The owners acknowledged increased business from appreciative residents, and neighbouring building owners caught the façade-improving spirit.

for a downtown project. Their ambivalence could be as fatal as outright opposition.

Key individuals and groups vary from town to town. In Moose Jaw, the Chamber of Commerce is the major business group, while in Perth, the Rotary Club and the Chamber of Commerce are particularly strong. Even so, in Perth the project relied heavily on Richard Schooley, a local insurance agent. He had the necessary leadership abilities and profile among the merchants to bring them together. The Main Street office developed a good rapport with Schooley since he was sympathetic to the goals of the project; his enthusiasm played a large part in the project's success.

Recruitment of the movers and shakers within a community can take a great deal of time. Certainly it does not happen overnight. Cambridge, Ontario, co-ordinator Don Macintosh estimated that for the first nine months most of his time was spent achieving exposure for the project and identifying the critical personalities within the city. Part of his problem was the sheer size of Cambridge, itself a recent amalgamation of the historical and traditional social centres of Galt, Hespeler, and Preston. Its social network, the informal fabric of the larger community, was far from defined in crisp and clear organizations. Rather, the friendships and contacts that spanned the various groups – some economic, some social, some cultural – described a delicate web.

The Players in the Game

While the informal fabric of a community can be subtle, there are none the less downtown groups that should be involved in the work of the Main Street revitalization. They fall into three broad categories: the institutional or public sector, especially the municipal and provincial governments which provide programs and grants; the private sector, including individual businesses and the collective business-improvement associations; and various community groups, such as heritage societies and service clubs. Each of these is essential to the success of a downtown project.

Institutional influences used to be clearly delineated, with the municipal government responsible for one level of local services while the province took initiatives on more general matters. Increasingly, however, there have been instances where the provincial agency defines the mandatory framework for any local action. This is especially so in the case of zoning, planning, and funding. By-laws that permit or prohibit particular land uses within or outside designated areas can be part of the official plan of a community, itself often nested within a broader official plan for the county or regional district. If Main Street is part of a broader provincial road system, changes in traffic-flow patterns, widening or narrowing the streets, and the placement of signs may all come under provincial-level controls concerning highway matters.

While funds for revitalization projects can be raised from local taxes, most major capital grants come through provincial agencies. The co-ordinator should be prepared to work with municipal officials to explore the potential of a wide variety of provincial funds. In Nova Scotia, for example, this would require establishing some liaison with the Department of Development and its Main Street program. In Windsor and Bridgetown the co-ordinators were able to tailor requests to the guidelines of that program; additionally, they were able to seize the opportunities presented by grants available to high-unemployment areas. Such grants had never been intended to help upgrade Main Street but, skilfully employed, helped to create work crews for painting, tree planting, sidewalk laying, and other labour-intensive tasks that would have dug into other funding totals. In Fort Macleod the Alberta Ministry of Culture wanted to give outright grants to Main Street property owners for restoration work. The merchants, however, wanted property owners to show financial commitment, so they recommended a cost-sharing approach. Clearly, they thought that personal commitment on the part of building owners would be an important part of the revitalization of Main Street. The project co-ordinator, as in other pilot towns, saw this as a healthy sign that local initiatives and local priorities were being articulated. The co-ordinator's role was not perceived to consist merely of continually seeking different sources of hand-outs.

In Nelson, negotiating grants for individual property owners or the entire downtown was a major activity of the downtown co-ordinator. The downtown has been almost completely refurbished through effective grantsmanship. In this case, the existence of a major plan (for all its controversy at the time) gave the town the necessary credibility with Victoria. The province and its agency, the British Columbia Heritage Trust, knew the purpose and context of any grant request. Nova Scotia's Main Street program similarly uses consultant advice to orchestrate the effective flow of funds to local communities. The downtown co-ordinator can play a critical role in guiding the local community through this bureaucratic maze.

The institutional sector plays one additional important role. The public-works department (for locality or province, depending on the jurisdiction) is responsible for the maintenance of all public property in the downtown. That department's role in keeping the downtown clean, ensuring the fast removal of snow, and completing repair work with minimum disruption is an important contribution to a smooth-running downtown project. Government is also a major landowner and employer. The town hall, library, and public-utility-commission offices are all high-activity areas. Provincially regulated activities, such as liquor or beer stores, are major downtown retail anchors. While a liquor store may cause problems of circulation and parking, its continuing presence on Main Street rather than in a new warehouse on the edge of town is desirable. Regional provincial offices and courthouses also generate activities which attract people. Their buildings are often among the most prominent and historic in the community. Funds geared to public-works maintenance or to rehabilitating heritage-designated buildings can enhance the downtown.

The co-ordinator has a responsibility to be involved with various administrations. Occasionally this may be at the level of permit applications for signs, buildings, parades, or special events. At other times it may be the drafting and monitoring of grant applications. A co-ordinator should be in a position to represent downtown interests on whatever municipal committees are discussing the downtown. He or she should also be aware of the appropriate and efficient paths to provincial departments and agencies. Since local government is a provincial responsibility, federal agencies are not directly of concern here. However, there are various programs related to unemployment or regional-economic development that can often be turned to advantage. Federal buildings such as post offices are also high-volume downtown anchors and historic landmarks. Their presence on Main Street can be critical.

The key to downtown improvement, whatever public-sector funds can be attracted, is the business community. The members of this group traditionally tend to emphasize the differences among themselves rather than their similarities. However, the co-ordinator must work closely with these groups to strengthen their organization and develop long-range goals. Most towns have a board of trade or a chamber of commerce. Since they draw membership from the edge of the community as well as the downtown, it is difficult to focus their attention on revitalizing the downtown. An organization such as a business-improvement association is needed. In Windsor, Nova Scotia, co-ordinator Chris Pelham spent more than a year trying to establish a business-improvement-district commission (BIDC) to co-ordinate improvements aimed at making the downtown more attractive to business. Support of 51 per cent of commercial taxpayers was needed before establishing a BIDC. Initially voted down, the proposal was accepted a year later, once the merchants realized the benefits of such an organization. With the

The hall of the Fraternal Order of the Eagles on Baker Street as the co-ordinators in Nelson first saw it (above left), 'slip-covered' in aluminum siding. Above right, the process of 'investigative demolition,' probing into the building's history of renovations, begins.

An archival photograph of Baker Street in 1960 shows the Eagles Hall with its original structural features intact.

The Eagles Hall denuded of several layers of earlier alterations. At this stage one is tempted to reapply aluminum siding.

below The Eagles Hall restored

OPPOSITE

top Baker Street in 1982

bottom By the summer of 1984 Baker Street had been transformed, thanks to the generous assistance of the province's Downtown Revitalization Program, the Heritage Area Revitalization Program, and the building owners. The Heritage Canada Foundation and the city supplied the co-ordination and design expertise.

The completed project in Nelson has become a handsome setting for annual events such as the International Bike Race sponsored by the Downtown Business Association.

province's Main Street program allocating funds only to towns with such commissions in place to look after the program's administration, Windsor would not otherwise have been able to take advantage of these possibilities. As it was, council set for 1983 a special business-improvement-district area rate of ten mills, to be levied as an additional tax on all real commercial property and on business-occupancy assessments in the downtown business district, in order to raise $8,746 for the BIDC operational budget. To this was added a $6,746 grant from town council, $23,240 from the province's Main Street program, and $53,600 from the federal NEED (New Employment Expansion and Development) program. All told, this gave the BIDC an operating budget of $92,332 in its first year. While granting agencies and business organizations are governed by slightly different relationships in other provinces, everywhere the key is, as it was in Windsor, to organize a specific downtown business identity. This same organization is then in place to pursue marketing studies, to co-ordinate special-events promotions, and to articulate collective opinions on a variety of planning issues at council meetings.

While an umbrella organization is vital, individual merchants and landlords must be involved as well. Downtowns are difficult to organize, due to the rugged individualism of the merchants and landlords. A solution for one downtown will not automatically work for another. The co-ordinator must treat each merchant individually and give special attention to his particular needs. This grass-roots, personalized approach will help to ensure that the messy vitality of downtown survives.

Merchants and landlords are the kingpins of any revitalization effort. It is they, rather than a heritage group, who are responsible for developing better business practices and an improved business image through upgraded façades and improvements to signs. In Nelson, Bob Inwood felt that a few critical businessmen were the conduit of effective support for a Baker Street revitalization. Among them were Lyle Hornby of Sterling's Home Furniture; Bud Darough, a real-estate dealer who owned the RHC building, which was the first to receive heritage treatment; David Martin, a hotelier who invested heavily to improve the inside of his building; and Dick Moulin, the acting president of the Downtown Business Association. It should also be pointed out that Bob Inwood and Hans Honegger joined the Nelson Fraternal Order of the Eagles in order to explore the possibilities of uncovering the original façade of the building in which the order met. Inwood and Honegger had seen the building's Victorian detailing on archival photographs and wondered whether it survived behind a 1950s aluminum façade. It did, and as members of the FOE they were able to approach the landlord

The Nelson Downtown Business Association extends an annual invitation to the Doukhobor choir to sing Russian Christmas carols on Baker Street, bringing even more life to the downtown.

Preparing lunch for the walkathon in Windsor, Nova Scotia. The Main Street office's support of the walk, which raised fifteen hundred dollars for downtown Christmas decorations, was an important first step in building local enthusiasm for the project.

with a proposal to restore its heritage façade, a restoration that would create a better retailing image for the ground-floor tenant. The lodge invested funds, and the downtown gained not only another heritage building but also another link in a revitalized Baker Street.

The media are another important private-sector group. Much of the decline of downtown is attitudinal. Attitudes can be changed when a well-briefed press informs the public of the downtown-revitalization project's improvements. Gordon Fulton, the Moose Jaw co-ordinator, felt that an important psychological threshold had been crossed when, after nine months, unprompted by him, editorials in the Moose Jaw *Times-Herald* began to rap knuckles when building plans seemed detrimental; the newspaper also publicized the positive impact of some of the heritage initiatives.

Among the various community groups whose support can be valuable are service clubs, sports clubs, and heritage societies. Service groups do not have the same kind of vested interest in the downtown as do the merchants. They are generally devoted, however, to bettering the community and are ready-made volunteer organizations that can widen community involvement with the downtown. Some of these groups will be larger and more effective than others, and since they are volunteer organizations, they should be given responsibilities commensurate with their abilities. But their participation can be mutually beneficial. As well as being the major location for retail and non-commercial services, the downtown is also the best location for community groups to stage activities. In order for a club to maintain a high profile, it needs to conduct its activities in front of as many people as possible. Fund-raising events, exhibitions, and sporting events can take place downtown. In Nelson, Honegger and Inwood encouraged the local cycling club to start and finish its twenty-eight-mile road race on the downtown's Baker Street. The office made all the arrangements with the city to close the streets. The result was hundreds of spectators, excellent exposure for the club, and another support activity for the downtown.

Local heritage and preservation groups can be valuable sources of design advice. They can also help with promotions based on a community's history. In all of the pilot projects, local heritage groups have been strong supporters. Yet a word of caution to potential co-ordinators: merchants and heritage groups traditionally do not see eye to eye on many issues. The historical role played by many heritage groups has been confrontational and argumentative. The co-ordinator must be cautious about how the heritage objectives are realized. Many people, especially merchants, fear that a Main Street program will turn their downtown into a museum. To counteract this perception the co-ordinator must emphasize the business approach to the project and reassure all citizens that the effective revitalization of the economy can go hand in hand with a healthy stock of heritage buildings.

Steps to Success

Possibly the biggest dilemma facing the co-ordinator, once he or she is in residence and has some sense of the critical players, is what to do first. While it is important not to suggest a game-plan for the project, the co-ordinator should certainly have some sense of organization. What ideally are the objectives? What changes in business design, image, promotion, and organization are desired? Once the co-ordinator has a sense of the town's physical stock, its economic track record, and its social ingredients, he or she can compare it with the essential ingredients of a 'successful' downtown. Can such a list be used to define the town's advantages, deficiencies, and potential? If so, it would help the co-ordinator to establish priorities.

The essential ingredients for a successful downtown include the same elements that combine to make a shopping mall successful:

Ease of access	Unified identity
Consumer choice	Positive image
Pleasant environment	Controlled design
Effective market analysis	Clear direction
Effective advertising	Effective management

The co-ordinator should identify the present state of each element in the life of the downtown area. The potential for improvement as well as the feasibility of improvement in each category should be considered. No two downtowns are identical. They have varying strengths and weaknesses. Most downtowns, however, will need improvement in each of these areas. The co-ordinator must establish for himself and for the project a priority list which balances areas in need of improvement with their potential and feasibility.

While the areas with the greatest need or the areas with the most seductive potential should not be disregarded, efforts should be concentrated on the achievement of realistic goals. Particularly during the first year, goals that can be easily realized in a short period of time should be attempted. Effective long-term gain will likely be simply the sum of these smaller parts. A major change, on one problem building or one block, might be feasible after two years of subtle suggestion have laid the groundwork and as two years' worth of change unfolds around

The 1984 Christmas parade in Fort Macleod, Alberta. The success of the first parade, organized by the Heritage Canada co-ordinator shortly after he arrived in the community, surprised and then galvanized the local business community, and the celebration has become a major regional event attracting large crowds.

The continuity of the Ferguson Block on Gore Street in Perth, Ontario, had been seriously broken up by irreverent façade alterations.

The Ferguson Block with a more harmonious sign and with happy second-floor
tenants, who rediscovered sunshine

the site. This neighbouring change can often speak more effectively than anything the co-ordinator can say.

In most of the pilot projects the initial activities of the co-ordinators were directed at special events or unified promotions. In Bridgetown the office co-ordinated a Firemen's Appreciation Day, which broke the ice for the project and introduced Peter Hyndman and Chris Pelham to all the merchants and many townspeople. This experience was matched in Windsor by a businessmen's walkathon to raise money for Main Street Christmas decorations. Despite two well-attended weddings in Bridgetown on the same day as the Firemen's Appreciation Day and the cold weather for the Windsor walkathon, the two events were successful. The Windsor walk raised fifteen hundred dollars. These were important first steps in building momentum for both projects.

As momentum developed in the Perth project, John Stewart waited for an opportunity to restore a building façade. From a chance meeting with a merchant he learned that Glen Girdwood at Girdwood's Drug Store was having some work done on his store-front. He rushed over to the store to see the hoarding being erected by the contractor. A few words with Glen, and the office was given its first chance at a façade redesign. This was the turning point for the entire project because merchants and landlords had a chance to see for themselves that a properly designed store-front could be affordable. After Girdwood's was completed, many more merchants asked for a design from the Main Street office.

In Fort Macleod, Jim Mountain got off to a flying start by organizing a Santa Claus parade, the first ever in the town and the only one in Alberta that year. The local business community was amazed at the response, and the media in Lethbridge and Calgary sat up and noticed. Beyond any immediate retail spin-off that day, the promotion indicated community support that could be tapped in future. Mountain's efforts to redesign store-fronts and launch other promotions could proceed with confident support rather than with nervous, let's-wait-and-see caution.

Tackling bite-sized pieces of the downtown problem is the basis of the incremental approach to downtown revitalization. It should be remembered that downtowns grew incrementally, lot by lot and building by building. Their success depended upon many individual contributions which, when combined, were greater than the sum of their individual parts. This kind of change maintains the character of downtown and in the long run is more beneficial and long-lasting than stitched-on, one-shot solutions. Incremental change requires and re-establishes the tradition of self-help.

In Perth, where the program began, one of the symbols of the impact of the Heritage Canada project was the removal of the old Beamish store sign. As in so many Ontario small towns, Perth's commercial rows had been severely cut up by façade alterations. The Ferguson block on Gore Street was one such example. A row of three-storey stores and apartments was hidden by a twenty- by sixty-foot sign that blocked out 90 per cent of the light entering the second storey. Discussions about the fate of this sign had gone on almost from the beginning of the project. Besides being ugly, the sign was also redundant, since Beamish no longer ran the store. Whether to pull the sign down and how to treat the store-front and fascia board in its absence occupied many hours of discussion and sketching in the Main Street office and with the new property owners. Finally, in the summer of 1983 the new owners volunteered to remove the sign. A new store-front, with appropriately scaled signs, replaced it. The building, the street, and, in a way, the entire downtown seemed to have a little more unity. All the individual store treatments and the sprucing up of the Bank of Montreal down the street tied that little bit together even more.

The 'magic' of this transformation is not magic at all, for it requires the marshalling and co-ordination of community resources which, for the most part, already exist. In Perth the transformation was more than physical. The self-confidence of the entire community took a leap forward. The resources of heritage architecture, beautiful natural setting, and the individual talents of people were already in the community. The town seemed to have been waiting for someone or some group from outside the community to tell it that what it possessed was unique and worth enhancing. The town responded with enthusiasm and hard work. The same boost in self-confidence has been witnessed in the other demonstration towns. It is the project's greatest result, since it will ensure that a concern for the preservation of the unique qualities in each community will continue to affect future development long after the project has been completed.

Many owners of buildings on Main Street have coped with problems by covering them over. Here a building in Perth, Ontario, has been given a new brick face, when a ten-dollar eavestrough could have prevented further moisture damage.

HANS HONEGGER and ROBERT INWOOD

Store-Fronts for Downtown

The store-fronts lining Canadian main streets contain a mix of architectural styles that are an important visual record of enterprise and culture. Many continue to serve their owners in the face of stiff competition. Unfortunately, flaking paint does not match the slick modern image of chrome to be found in shopping malls. Even worse, elegant old upper façades peering across pastiched attempts at modernization sometimes seem like pathetic clowns vying for attention. Old buildings need not be embarrassments to their owners. Good historical architecture, properly cared for, has an intrinsic worth that can be of economic benefit as a marketing tool. The building needn't be a gem or a landmark. Many ordinary buildings contribute to eye-catching streetscapes.

The old commercial buildings on Main Street can be improved. The results demonstrate positive physical change and are signals that new life is being breathed into the downtown. For a business community embarking on a program that will be several years in execution, minor changes to store-front appearance can be a good short-term goal until longer-term initiatives begin to bear fruit. In time, as more buildings have attention paid to façades and store-fronts, the cumulative effect can be startling.

Framework and Canvas

A very simple framework enables the viewer to read a building. Commercial architecture on Main Street, no matter what period or style, is made up of three basic segments: store-front, upper façade, and cornice.

The store-front, at the pedestrian level, is designed to display consumer goods. Many variations on the specific placement of glass and structural members have evolved over the years, altering with changes in marketing concepts and technological advances in building materials. Structurally, the upper façade is supported by store-front columns or posts upholding a horizontal beam. The fill inside this structural system constitutes the aesthetic shop-front. The lower portion, usually referred to as the bulkhead, consists of a short 'knee wall' which supports the picture windows. Doors are often inset, largely to prevent them from swinging out into the faces of passing pedestrians. At the same time, an inset door allows additional display glass. The transom area, over the doors and windows, can be given a variety of opaque or translucent finishes. It provides a considerable amount of indirect lighting for the store interior.

The upper façade is a mass of one or more additional storeys. Upper-floor space can be devoted to diverse uses, most typically to additional mercantile space, offices, meeting rooms, or living suites. (Even if a store is essentially a one-storey structure, it will most likely have an upper façade, hiding the gable roof and giving the illusion of a two-storey building.) Upper-façade detailing includes window openings (sometimes fake), window surrounds, and surface treatments that are variously plain or elaborate, depending on their period of construction.

The cornice marks the termination of the building with the sky and, as befits this grand juncture, has traditionally been treated with great flourish. Specific cornice types are as indicative of particular stylistic trends as are all the other parts of a building. The cornice also serves an important weather-proofing function by protecting the roof and façade materials from intruding water.

With these basic building components as given, the skin of the structure becomes a canvas of sorts, reflecting the artistic temperament and technological innovations of the passing decades. Most Main Street buildings are less than 150 years old. Most have a simple balance, in so far as upper-floor window openings are symmetrical and often present a pleasing rhythm as an ensemble on a street-block. Through the nineteenth century, the upper-floor windows and cornice received more decorative attention, with elaborate bracketing holding up the cornice, stamped metal or stone lintels, and other window trim, all of which gave the façade a more three-dimensional quality. From the 1920s to the 1940s a more streamlined façade, often known as art deco, made more of smooth surfaces, geometric patterns, and shiny materials for impact.

Since the Second World War automobiles have caused a profound

The Littlewood building on Baker Street in Nelson, British Columbia, before restoration

As the basic elements of a façade reappeared, the structural integrity of the Littlewood building emerged. The cornice has been painted and its details highlighted. The store-front, with its cast-metal supporting columns, has become more coherent, its bulkhead stripped and cleaned of the patio-stone veneer.

Local materials have often been used to produce the simplest and most elegant finishing details. Here a wooden cornice with brackets, a feature typical of many western buildings, lends grandeur to a modest structure in Fort Macleod, Alberta.

right This stamped-metal cornice in Kaslo, British Columbia, was prefabricated in the east, then transported by train and delivered by stern-wheeler. It was evidently intended for a much taller structure. Many late-nineteenth-century buildings could be assembled part by part from catalogues.

A rhythmic terra-cotta cornice in Moose Jaw, Saskatchewan

The L&S Supermarket on Main Street in Moose Jaw, Saskatchewan, with its stucco surfaces, rounded corners, glass block, horizontal lines, and strip neon, typifies the influence of art deco on many Main Street buildings dating from the 1930s and 40s.

change in a building's visual role on the street. Victorian designers saw their creations as tangible symbols of the virtues their clients wished to express to the public. With shoppers in cars, modern design and advertising techniques preach that the merchant's sign is the focus of all the attention and the building it rests on should be as unobtrusive as possible. Owners of older eclectic buildings, finding themselves dangerously out of sync with the current trend, have frequently endeavoured to create a modern image by blanking out the venerable symbolic façade. Often this was an overlay rather than wholesale replacement, and the original lies behind. Now that downtowns are again being seen as places to walk and shop and sit rather than simply to drive through, many designers and merchants are returning to a store-front appearance that distinguishes and highlights store-front, façade, and cornice.

A Spring Cleaning for Old Buildings

A Main Street co-ordinator offering design advice to merchants and property owners is faced with the challenge of sorting out the confused personality of Main Street one building at a time. Some buildings are denuded of detail and others totally resheathed with inappropriate veneers. The intention is to retrieve some of the former glory of these structures and to reinforce the visual relatedness of these buildings to their neighbours. Most of the examples that follow are drawn from the authors' experience in Nelson, British Columbia, although equally good examples could as easily have been drawn from other regions in Canada.

At the outset it is important to stress that buildings often do not need large amounts of money poured into them to make them look good. Nor should there be a worry that a building has to be restored to the exact condition it enjoyed the day it was built. The Comic Shop in Nelson, for example, required minimal alteration and a minimal budget of about five hundred dollars. The intent was not to attempt a full-scale restoration but to give the store dynamic impact on the street. The challenge was to alter the façade to reflect the tenant's business, refraining, however, from undertaking alterations to the building. The owner could foresee restoring the 1890s wood-frame structure at a later date. A decision was also made at the outset to maintain the vinyl siding, since it was in good condition.

An air-conditioner, needed to solve the problem of overheating in the store, was a visually disturbing façade element. Awnings were discussed and rejected as being too expensive. With the air-conditioner repaired and therefore a permanent feature, the design solution was

Sterling Home Furnishings in Nelson, British Columbia, before restoration. During the 1950s and 60s throughout North America, shrouding building façades and focusing instead on the business sign was thought to project a more 'modern' image.

Sterling's with the metal siding removed. The original surfaces suggest a genuine and timeless sophistication simply because they are more durable.

directed at making it less visually disturbing. Viewed as an objective, what had begun as an obstacle became an opportunity. A plywood sign was made in the shape of a car filled with comic-book characters, and the air-conditioner became the grille. The primary colours of comic books are to be used further in a paint scheme. A yellow door and red trim will create a co-ordinated image.

Many buildings in the eastern and central parts of Canada, as well as in the West, are simple two-storey structures sandwiched between more imposing buildings on the street. In the fifties and sixties they were easy targets for small amounts of aluminum siding that covered the upper-floor windows and cornice. The Griffith Bicycle Shop in Cambridge, Ontario, for example, could be returned to a more attractive appearance with minimal effort, as the Jeans and Joggers shop in Windsor, Nova Scotia, has been. There, a mid-cornice and a new upper cornice were boxed in with plywood, and all of a sudden there is a smart 'new' building on the street. Colour choices, in this case a slate grey for the wood and a sandstone yellow for the cornice, suggest a far more sturdy and substantial building than is the case. This was attained for a mere six hundred dollars.

In Nelson, the Annable block is a two-storey commercial row built on a sloping street. Stores at the lower end have a far greater area of subfloor, bulkhead, and transom space between the sidewalk and the mid-cornice line that spans the row. Over the years, the surrounds of the display windows in each store had been treated differently, and there was a clutter of materials, awnings, and signs. The architectural quality of this modest building was hidden. The intention was minimal rehabilitation (budget: twelve thousand dollars), to provide a crisp new image to six ground-level store-fronts; to replace existing canopies with ones of a more sympathetic nature; and to provide a clean and respectable image for second-floor tenants. The building was stripped of all non-original veneers and textures, and the brick was cleaned with mild chemicals and water. The original transom windows were liberated and, where missing, were recreated with plywood and mouldings. A paint scheme was suggested that expressed the structural bays, separating each shop, highlighting decorative features, and harmonizing with the new awnings. The colour and geometry of the awnings were chosen with the aid of historical documentation. The awnings provided the necessary shade while serving as a setting for compatible signs positioned on the valances.

One of the problems discussed in earlier chapters is the impact of chain stores on the local Main Street. In the Hipperson's Home Hardware building in Nelson, the problem was how to create a clean new

Vinyl siding covers a boom-town row that houses the Comic Shop in Nelson.

The exposed air conditioner, once considered an eyesore, was turned into a playful opportunity – and a low budget became a chance for the merchant and designer to exercise creativity and resourcefulness.

Minimal effort could improve this building in Cambridge, Ontario. What is behind the vegetable-grater siding?

image for a national chain hardware store recently located in town. Situated on a corner site, the modern building did not fit easily with its older brick and stone neighbours. It had been built without a cornice, with large horizontal upper-storey windows, and finished with a stucco surface. Several goals were identified. One was to diminish the horizontal look of the second-floor addition and to harmonize this structure with neighbouring older buildings. Another was to decrease the projection distance of the existing canopy (to allow clearance for new streetlights that the city was installing) while still providing sidewalk protection. Other goals were to discourage vandalism of signs and to incorporate signs identifying the chain store while maintaining the identity of the owner-manager. Lastly, it was necessary to increase the weathertightness of front doors and windows. All this had to be done so as to interfere as little as possible with business.

All disruptive work was done on Sundays. All unnecessary signs and clutter were stripped off, and stucco was patched and painted. To address the streetscape issue, a three-tone paint scheme was applied in a geometric pattern that was vertically oriented. At the skyline the building was painted a dark colour, matching the awning, to suggest a cornice which terminated the structure. The Home Hardware sign was relocated over the central entrance, adding to its visibility and vandalproofing. New awnings, with the owner's identification painted on, were installed. Awnings had a diminished projection but were hung lower to afford the same degree of protection as the originals. Finally, new doors and windows, colour co-ordinated with anodized aluminum siding and a painted plinth-dado, were installed. The total cost was fourteen thousand dollars. The Baker Street frontage is eye-catching, as is the bright expanse along the extensive side exposure. The completed redecoration of this building serves Home Hardware well as dramatic advertising.

A major renovation was attempted on Norm's Sports Centre. The entire building had been almost totally stripped of architectural features. Originally, this had been one of Nelson's more prominent commercial structures, with an elaborate corner tower and projecting bay windows. A 1950s set of big picture windows had replaced this focal point. Sandblasting had been done, and a maintenance-free covering of plasticized paint had been added. Much of the inferior brick, once hidden behind a cornice, was falling on to the sidewalk. Exposed roof rafters and floor joists were beginning to rot. Work on this building was essential to prevent further deterioration of brick surfaces (to avoid a lawsuit) and to arrest further decay to structural elements such as exposed roof rafters. Beyond these maintenance issues, the challenge was to make the

Jeans and Joggers in Windsor, Nova Scotia, before façade improvements

Jeans and Joggers with its new cornices and paint. With its missing details replaced, the upper façade not only looks but also weathers better.

second and third floors appealing to new tenants, to defray the necessary costs of reconstruction, and to identify the ground-level shop in a more tasteful manner.

The first step was to strip off all vinyl and aluminum surfaces that were disguising maintenance problems. Several functional components, such as parapet cornice, ground-level cornice, and projecting window pediments, were reapplied to the building. Their removal earlier had contributed significantly to the deterioration because it allowed water to run down and into the front wall. All projecting surfaces were given adequate flashings. Balconies were created at the corner, balancing the building visually, and alluding to previous grandeur while improving the rentability of the upper floors. A sympathetic multicoloured paint scheme was applied to highlight architectural features (cornice panels, pedimented windows, and so on). At the ground floor, vinyl was replaced with plywood and pine panels reminiscent of previous transom windows. Awnings created visual interest for the gound-level shop and assisted in shading windows. The budget here was $25,000.

A more elaborate restoration involved the Bank of Montreal in Perth, Ontario, which intended to modernize its building. It was built of stone, which presented problems of how to restore both the overall surface and the detail. There were certain design considerations having to do with access to the bank, the location of a night-deposit box, and the like. The co-ordinators criticized the original design by architects Ogilvie and Hogg and presented them with cartoon sketches of how it might look with minimal change, or as a pure restoration, or with a modified front. The architects changed their design, agreeing to work towards a treatment that respected the building and the street. Heritage Canada identified a local stonemason and found out where there were quarries cutting stone that matched the originals. The co-ordinators met with the contractors and discussed the glazing patterns (to avoid mirrored glass). The result was more than just a restored building. The project helped the bank stand behind a new logo – 'the bank that saves more than money.' There was public interest in the building, and the restoration became part of a marketing strategy.

Dialogue and several draft sketches of possible solutions – whether developed with a local independent, a national-chain manager, or a national bank – can help bring new life to old buildings. In the Nelson case, of course, generous grants from the provincial government for building rehabilitation undoubtedly made the job easier. There is growing evidence, however, that even without those funds a rehabilitated building can be more effective than demolition and replacement with some functional but uninspiring structure.

The Annable Block in Nelson, British Columbia, during renovation. The glass transom windows had been removed when ceilings were lowered to accommodate modern heating, air-conditioning, and lighting requirements.

The geometry of transom windows can be recreated with mouldings and paint. Awnings will be mounted to solve overheating and window-display problems.

The Annable Block as the Nelson co-ordinators first saw it, sheathed in grim, corrugated fibreglass and vinyl

The Annable Block cleaned of its clutter, now with expressed store bays and co-ordinated colours. Old photographs were used as guides to the choice of awnings.

Hipperson's Home Hardware in Nelson, with
poorly placed and easily vandalized signs and
inappropriate corrugated fibreglass awnings

Hipperson's with its new awning and paint, and its
sign relocated over the main entrance

The blankness of the expansive side wall of Hipperson's Hardware was accentuated by its 1960s-vintage horizontal windows.

Paint was used to create a bolder cornice on Hipperson's and an illusion of verticality more in harmony with the style of the store's Victorian neighbours. The combined effect of design and setting makes the building appear to soar.

Norm's Sports Centre in Nelson before renovation. Behind the plasticized paint and aluminum, original surfaces and structural elements had reached a critical stage of decay.

Artist's conception of Norm's Sports Centre at the turn of the century, developed from the photograph of Baker Street in 1896 that appears on page 146. Note the parapet cornice, second-floor cornice, and cast-iron supports at ground level.

The third-floor balcony restored

Exposed rafter ends are covered with a replacement cornice.

Norm's Sports Centre with some of its missing features replaced. The new cornice prevents further deterioration of the roof-rafter ends, and the balconies are an attraction to future tenants.

The Bank of Montreal in Perth, Ontario, its façade disguised by roof-level and first-storey modernist alterations

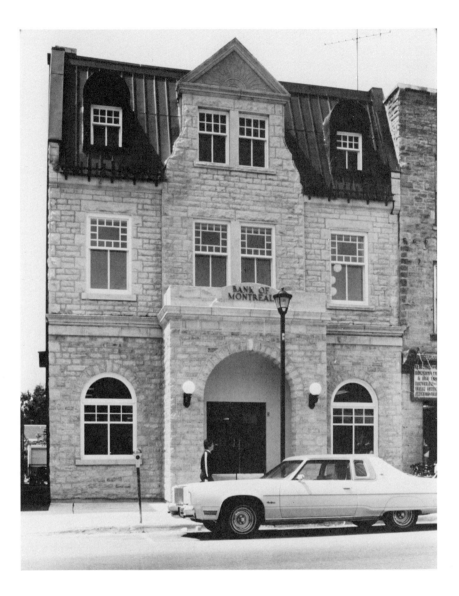

With its original structural details freed, the bank appears to advance with dignity towards the street, justified in its new marketing claim that it is 'the bank that saves more than money.'

Two background themes pervade the examples discussed above. One is a sense of how the building used to look; the other, how its elements served maintenance as well as design functions. Together, they accord with what for centuries have been the architect's priorities. The Roman writer Vitruvius said that architecture should possess the qualities of firmness (be structurally sound), commodity (be spatially functional), and delight (be aesthetically pleasing). These qualities remain to this day the governing directives, regardless of whether the project involves new construction, restoration, or renovation. Some of the ways in which a co-ordinator can advance these ideals and also interact with professional architects and contractors are summarized in the following section.

Above-Ground Archaeology

The Nelson examples clearly suggest that the building itself and its rich history offer opportunities for revitalization. Rarely do we have to invent history. Revitalization is, instead, a question of knowing what is there and how to find it.

One of the most important first steps to take when confronted with an historical building in any state of disrepair is to research its visual history. Old photographs, sketches, and paintings can yield invaluable clues to the nature of the original building façade and the changes it has undergone. Written documentation that can help to tie down the period of construction and initial use can be found in local museums, provincial archives, newspaper backfiles, and municipal records of land titles. Plumbing records, indicating when water was first supplied to the building, often act as useful dating surrogates. Fire-insurance atlases, if available, record the various building materials originally used and may give clues as to what lies behind a recent change. Elderly area residents can often prove most helpful in rounding out the historical profile of a given property.

After amassing as much historical data as possible, one should try to develop a complete understanding of the building's past metamorphoses. What was the architectural style of the original façade? Base photographs should be taken from all available angles in both colour slides and black and white prints. Photos are important not only as bench-marks in the project flow but also as useful design tools – a slide projected on to a piece of paper can then be traced. This gives a rough sense of relative proportions. In order to get an accurate photo image, use a perspective-corrected lens or try to remove perspective distortion by finding a straight-on elevational angle, such as from an upper-storey window of a building across the street or, failing that, from a car roof. The placement of some physical scale-markers on the face of the building – at some known increment such as a foot or a metre – can later be used to establish a sense of scale on the photographic prints and help fill in the details of the elevation drawing (the brick, glass, or siding dimension can help here).

The building should also be physically examined in some detail. Rear façades of buildings often contain considerable information about past renovations. A trip into the basement should yield insights into the building's structural system. The upper floors might show earlier windows now blocked in or covered over, and a visit to the roof reveal the soundness of weather-proofing.

It is often necessary to make decisions regarding a building's condition and proposed restoration without stripping away all of the accretions that hide the actual façade. Detective work can reveal numerous clues as to the store-front's state of repair. Proceeding from a basic knowledge of the elements of a building façade, the co-ordinator should undertake an assessment of the condition or absence of typical façade elements. Look specifically for missing elements such as cornice bands above the shop-front, prominent roof cornices, door and window trim, and pediments. Scar marks of removed trim and ornament can often be seen outlined subtly by accumulated dust or paint-colour changes. A close look at the edges of exposed veneer materials in cross-section may tell much about the nature of the original materials hidden beneath more recent renovations. Such careful investigations may often yield enough data for the co-ordinator to begin to work up a feasible design proposal for the building, and the owner may now be prepared to allow a more thorough look at the property's hidden secrets.

'Investigative demolition' is the careful process of probing into the building's history of renovations by stripping off the crust of more recent renovations and examining the historical fabric underneath. The key to successful archaeology, even at this pedestrian scale, is to be as organized and thorough as possible. Field notes are valuable, especially when keyed to photo documentation or field drawings. Tools for the process are fairly simple. Pry bars, hacksaws (for sawing nails to protect woodwork), awls for testing the firmness of wood, and a matte knife for taking paint samples make up a good basic kit. One should proceed carefully, removing as little original material as possible. Analysing paint slices can help to establish the building's true historical colouring. After a sample slice has been taken, ideally from some protected area such as some trim or an eave, the sample can be viewed in cross-section under a 10–20x magnification. Such considerations as the possibility of paint fading and the dark (dirt) layers that indicate successive paintings should be kept in mind.

After the building has been researched, the final documentation process can begin. Accurate as-found drawings, showing the building before renovation work begins, are valuable parts of any design process. They document for posterity the condition of the building and also give the designer accurate data from which to develop a restoration plan. Plan and elevational views should be drawn to scale, with special ornamental details elaborated upon. Measurements should be taken of all vertical and horizontal dimensions of the building, usually by working to prominent architectural features such as doors and window openings, cornices, and transoms. Keeping the plan and elevation to the same scale and arranging the drawings physically one on top of another on tracing vellum can help when the dimensions are correlated on paper. The as-found drawings may then be turned over to a designer who is to develop a plan for the building's rehabilitation. Several solutions for shop-front, signboard, or even paint schemes can be quickly overlaid in tracings and can give the merchant or owner a sense of what the finished product will look like. This process does not take place in isolation, of course, and should be lined up alongside what is known of neighbouring buildings. Before any Main Street design work is begun, all of downtown should be systematically photographed. This includes shots taken in the four directions at every intersection and frontal shots of every building. Sunday morning tends to be a good time for such work, as there is little traffic and there are few parked cars to interfere with store-front lines.

Maintenance

Several of the steps taken in renovating specific Nelson buildings were made necessary simply because of the previous poor maintenance of those buildings. Details that are difficult to reach are more prone to decay. This should be kept in mind when replacements are being designed. Care should be taken to ensure their longevity. Flashing details are critical. Imagine water flooding down the façade. Wherever water might drip, blow, or settle, those areas should be protected. Wooden areas should be protected with impermeable surfaces, such as painted aluminum and galvanized flashing; masonry, with flashings of canted plasticized mortar.

Most Main Street design work is not an additive process but one that requires the removal of accumulated surfaces, whether siding, paint, stucco, or just grime. No new surface is as durable and as honest as the original building material. Adding new surfaces over old only cheapens

the integrity of a building and creates yet another maintenance problem. The prime goal of a design scheme is to minimize maintenance
requirements by relying on the quality of the original materials and by
making the building perform and weather better. Cleaning can be a
tricky and dangerous process, however. A co-ordinator should be able
to offer informed guidance about appropriate methods, and a series of
helpful pamphlets is available from Heritage Canada's Ottawa head office. As the following general guidelines suggest, though, the first
step in the process should be to contact an experienced building-exterior
cleaner.

The various materials that compose a façade must be considered when
a cleaning program is being developed. Sheet metal and cast iron are
elements that possess a quality of permanence if adequately painted to
prevent corrosion. Accumulated paint and rust can be easily removed
by chemicals or low-pressure dry-grit blasting at 80–100 psi (552–690
kPa) for tenacious areas. Stamped-metal details that approximate the
look of wood are often quite thin; sand-blasting should be avoided on
such surfaces since it can perforate them. Always ensure that these
details are adequately fastened, painted, and caulked. This prevents
moisture from penetrating the wooden backing and prevents further
corrosion.

Masonry, both brick and stone, has an intrinsic longevity. Moisture
usually is the primary cause of its deterioration. Clogged or broken
eavestroughs and drain pipes should be repaired. Repointing of masonry
joints is a necessity. The mortar mix should match the original in both
consistency and colour; in cases where the former is in doubt, the mix
should be softer than the original (that is, contain less cement). A hard
mortar mix (high cement content) can prevent the evaporation of moisture in the walls and will reroute the moisture through the face of the
masonry, causing spalling (or flaking) of the surface during cycles of
freeze and thaw. High cement content in the mortar can also crack
brick, or even stone, which is softer than the binding agent.

The co-ordinator should try to ensure that abrasive cleaning methods
such as sand-blasting are never used on brick. Often non-ionic deter-
gents and bristle brushes are sufficient. For tougher cleaning projects
on reasonably sound brick, low-pressure water-cleaning at approximately 600 psi (4140 kPa) may be necessary. Heavy dirt on brick and
painted brick surfaces can be successfully cleaned with chemicals, but
always do test patches in hidden areas first. Chemicals may be alkaline
or acid or organic, but acid cleaners should never be used on buildings that have limestone or marble elements. Some chemicals perform
best under higher temperatures, and smaller amounts will be required

This 1896 photograph of Baker Street in Nelson, British Columbia, became an invaluable documentary source for the design conception of four restored façades in this row. The tower at the end is Norm's Sports Centre.

The Kootenay Exchange, an exchange and antiques business, had taken over the old Nelson Grocery building and its neighbour, the last remaining wood-sided structures on Baker Street. Old photographs first roused the curiosity of the Nelson co-ordinators, and set them to investigating what might remain under the stucco veneer.

top The Kootenay Exchange unmasked, and a wealth of clues laid bare that would help to guide in its reconstruction

The Kootenay Exchange fully recreated, down to a new coat of paint that duplicates the original colours.

left Paint scars indicate missing cornice brackets.

right Dust and discoloration had left graphic clues for the precise recreation of missing details.

The south side of the 300 Block on Baker Street in Nelson, 1981

The 300 Block in the winter of 1983

during warmer months. Be aware also that buildings cleaned in early spring or late fall can be seriously damaged by freezing, for masonry must be water-saturated to remove chemical cleaner.

Some softer bricks were historically painted as a means of protection. These surfaces should be repainted. Before they are, a light cleaning might be necessary to allow for sufficient bonding of the new paint. Use only a quality masonry paint which will allow the brick to retain its breathing qualities. An impermeable skin will create a moisture barrier, again causing spalling of the masonry face.

Proper treatment of wood is more obvious. Rotting pieces should be replaced. Those areas prone to moisture deterioration should be adequately flashed with either galvanized metal or aluminum sheeting. Missing elements should be repaced with milled lumber that matches the original. Often the planing bits are still available at custom woodworking shops. Always use a prime coat and then finish with two coats of a good-quality exterior paint. Gloss surfaces tend to weather better and gather less dust than low-lustre finishes. The difference between the longevity of a three-dollar-a-litre and an eight-dollar-a-litre paint can be ten years.

The majority of design solutions for façade treatments on Main Street tend to be simple repainting schemes. Colour can be used to highlight interesting architectural features and to harmonize discordant elements. It is the least expensive manner of both achieving drama and highlighting the personality of a structure. For historical authenticity, paint samples can be optically magnified and analysed from flake samples that have been taken from the trim of siding. Catalogues on historical paint schemes are available, as are books on contemporary approaches.

The pilot projects of the Heritage Canada Foundation's Main Street program can serve as source material for any design challenge. Historical research, careful knowledge of both the overall structure and its details, and a clear sense of the owner's financial limits and functional needs all contribute to an effective revitalization of Main Street buildings.

A sign that said it all in Macleod, Alberta

GORDON FULTON

Catching the Customer's Eye

Along commercial strips on the outskirts of most Canadian towns and cities, the motorist is confronted by a forest of bright signs and billboards announcing fast-food restaurants, gas stations, furniture stores, or any of a score of other shopping opportunities. Many national or international franchises count on the instant recognition of the distinctive shape, colour, or lettering of such signs. The signs are large enough to be read at a distance, helping the potential consumer to make decisions and choices long before he has to slow down and turn out of the flow of traffic. Many of those same illuminated signs, oriented to the fast-moving car driver, can be found downtown as well. There, however, they are not perched on top of fifty-foot-high poles at the edge of a parking lot; they are attached to the store-front, often obliterating the architectural façade behind the sign.

How to catch the customer's eye on Main Street without damaging the commercial viability of stores or the physical attractiveness of the streetscape is a problem that continually faces those hoping to revitalize downtown. In this chapter some examples of appropriate and inappropriate signs are examined, and the thorny matter of sign control is reviewed. We begin with an historical overview, since an understanding of changes in the art and science of sign-making can aid in the attainment of a mix and balance in the current streetscape.

An Historical Overview of Downtown Signs

The sign has been an integral part of business for centuries. It was usually incumbent on merchants in a given district to advertise their existence with signs since, without a public identity, they would have to rely on word of mouth to promote their trades. A sign was and is an extremely efficient means to call attention to oneself or one's trade.

With the emergence of the modern downtown in the last century, a unique identity took on added importance. By the mid-nineteenth century many downtowns had become highly concentrated collections of businesses, social organizations, and town amenities. It was not unusual, therefore, to have more than one business dealing in the same goods or services located near another. A unique identity for each specific business was required and was most often created by the use of the proprietor's name for both business and sign. The result was a profusion of signs which proclaimed the names of the owners in bold-face, very often omitting any description of their trades. Hitchcock & McCulloch or J. Robert et fils was considered adequate identification for a business. The social network in most small towns and cities and the supplementary advertising in newspapers and other printed media meant that it was not necessary for Messrs Hitchcock and McCulloch to spell out their type of business on their sign.

Soon, however, merchants began looking more critically at the effectiveness of their advertising, including their signs. In the larger towns with more mobile and transient populations, simple name association was no longer adequate. Even in the smaller centres, keener competition created by either improving or worsening economic conditions fostered a more aggressive business climate. More noticeable signs were becoming part of all but the most laggardly business communities. The downtown signscape of the late nineteenth century became very strident. In fact, the overriding image of many business districts of that period is one of signs, not buildings and streets. Signs covered entire walls, windows, and architectural elements. No space would be considered too trivial to warrant passing over by the sign-painter. A façade was often treated as a blank canvas for the sign-maker, particularly in the false-fronted pioneer west.

Restoration and renovation efforts of the last few decades have fostered a distorted view of the reality of the late-Victorian streetscape. 'Restorations' tend to clean up or sanitize items which may prove offensive to current aesthetics. This often includes uncluttering the downtown signscape by simplifying design elements or reducing the number or size of signs on a building. This approach, while not truly restoration, is acceptable, provided the result is not promoted as a facsimile of the nineteenth century. It is a reinterpretation of an era, accurate in some details, inaccurate in others. This approach poses certain basic

Water Street, St John's, Newfoundland, circa 1885 – the bold-faced approach to business identification

Talbot Street West, Leamington, Ontario, in 1910. Growth and aggressive promotion downtown led to a cacophony of signs by the turn of the century.

questions. Is an attempt being made to recreate a period image? And is it advisable to eradicate some tangible piece of downtown history by removing existing signs? The answers to these questions are at the heart of the overall revitalization plan – signage is but one component of the larger picture, and should be consistent with the revitalization framework.

We have already seen that the removal of an oversized and out-of-date sign in Perth helped dramatically to draw attention to the attractive upper-storey streetscape. Alternatively, retention of an old sign may enhance an historical sense. In Windsor, Nova Scotia, for example, a faded Coca-Cola sign, painted on an otherwise undistinguished side wall on Water Street, contributed a visual focus at one entrance to downtown. A new coat of paint has brought the 'ghost sign' to life, and it enhances the view along the street.

Technological Changes

The image and style of signs changed during the nineteenth century, but the materials and methods of producing them did not. Traditional materials, familiar to sign-makers in the previous two centuries, were being used in traditional ways by Victorian sign-makers. Wood, metal, glass, and paint were the standard stock of the trade. Like many other trades, however, the craft of sign-making began to be affected around the turn of the century by the rapid changes in available technology. These technological innovations, some material, some mechanical, had a profound impact on the craft. Both the sign-maker and the business person were quick to see the possibilities of the new technologies. Two advantages in particular caught their imagination and subsequently changed the nature of signs. The practical application of electricity and the refinement of materials and engineering principles heralded the modern era of sign-making.

More than any other single technological change, the use of electricity to light signs and to create self-lighted signs altered the appearance of the downtown signscape. Thomas Edison's demonstration of the first commercially practical light bulb in 1879 opened the door to untold creative lighting possibilities. In 1900 the prototype illuminated sign, a series of bare light bulbs surrounding a circular, oval, or rectangular panel two or three feet long, was developed. Advertising cards placed within the panels could be changed as required. The entire assembly was intended to be used as a window or interior display.

It did not take long for the effectiveness of a glittering sign to be recognized. Exterior application followed in short order. Both new electric

A tangible piece of the visual history of Windsor, Nova Scotia, was recaptured when this ghost sign was repainted in 1984.

The electric sign circa 1902. From this humble beginning came today's riot of light.

A large electric sign was an integral part of architect R.G. Bunyard's 1919 design for the Bellamy Company building in Moose Jaw, Saskatchewan.

Twentieth-century technology applied to signs: a name spelled out in lights and suspended far over a Vancouver sidewalk, circa 1910

illumination of traditional sign types and purpose-built electric signs became part of the lexicon of the sign-maker. In the latter category, the use of light bulbs to spell out names or messages gained widespread popularity in the early years of the twentieth century. The attraction of having one's business name spelled out in lights also dovetailed perfectly with the capabilities of neon lighting. This lighting used neon gas to produce red, helium gas to produce a yellowish white, and a mercury arc to produce blue. The development of fluorescent-coated glass tubing in the 1930s made a wide range of brilliant colours available, further popularizing the neon sign. The art of the tube benders would go into eclipse in later years, but it has recently been staging a come-back.

Great strides were being made at the same time in understanding and applying new engineering principles. Combined with newly developed materials, particularly man-made substitutes for natural or traditional materials, this evolution in engineering had a significant impact on the appearance of signs. The search for affordable materials with improved weathering and appearance properties led to the development of successful substitutes, notably of metals such as aluminum and of facing materials such as structural glass (Vitrolite and Carrara glass). The search also littered downtown with inferior products which did not match their predecessors in quality or appearance.

The result of these technological changes in the early twentieth century was, for the most part, our present signscape. Many well-designed, well-executed signs were built using the new technology of electricity and new principles of engineering and material substitution. These signs should be considered an integral part of the downtown's layering of history. Problems arose, however, when the technology overwhelmed the business, building, or street. There were few limits on what could be successfully attached to a building and called a sign. Engineering a sign to project ten feet or more over a sidewalk became possible – and inevitable – at an early date in this century. But whereas the first local attempt at this feat might be historically important, subsequent repetitions have been disruptive to the character of the street.

In many ways the question of appropriateness is a relative one. In the East, these signs were usually grafted on to an existing building; in the West and North, because of the later development period, a new building may have been designed with a larger projecting electric sign as an integral element. Decisions as to the suitability of keeping these signs should not be arbitrary. They should be based on an understanding of the context in which any given sign was installed. New sign designs should also take into account the local historical quirks, tastes, and technological sophistication in signs.

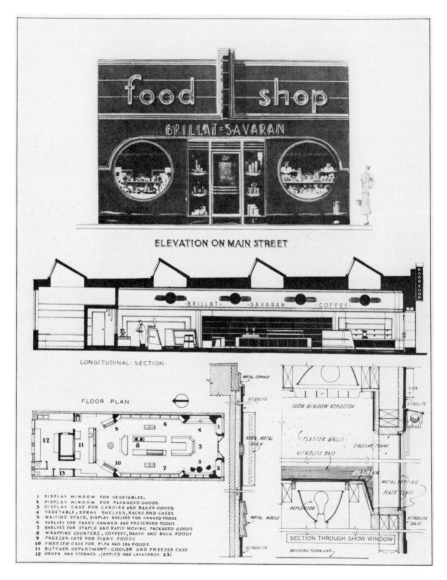

The 'Modernize Main Street' competition held by the *Architectural Record* magazine in 1935 helped architects to recast their notions about the relationship between buildings and their signs.

A well-crafted but almost illegible sign

A sign needlessly overscaled for its building

Too much information is as ineffective as too little.

Mass-produced signs often misrepresent or ignore entirely the building and business they are supposed to identify.

Aesthetic Changes

While electrical and engineering advances changed the downtown signscape by introducing new variables into the sign equation, aesthetic changes in the twentieth century have been simply a continuation of a long-running evolution. This century has, however, been marked by more dramatic shifts in popular taste than was the case in the nineteenth century. A more mobile population with more access to the popular press (itself capitalizing on its newly acquired ability to illustrate its texts extensively) has tended to latch on to trends, fashions, and fads more quickly than did its Victorian predecessors. There are three notable twentieth-century fashion or lifestyle changes that have had a great impact on the appearance of downtown signs.

The most important single feature affecting the appearance of Main Street has been the arrival of the motor car. The faster pace of automobile travel demanded a more brash presentation of product than had previously been necessary. This one fact of twentieth-century life – a world seen at thirty miles per hour – created a whole new aesthetic for signs. Typefaces and layouts were increasingly tailored to the fleeting view afforded automobile passengers. The ornamentation, flourishes, and intricate detail of the high-Victorian era were unsuited to this new condition. Lettering styles were simplified and emboldened, and subtleties of message and design were lessened. Along with the ubiquitous car came a new sophistication in advertising, influencing the nature of layout and design, illustration and typography. The changes in typography played an important role in the design evolution of signage. *Progressive* and *modern*, important terms in automotive and architectural fields, became important typographical concepts. Sanserif and unornamented typefaces began to dominate progressive design work, including signage, in the 1920s and 1930s.

The second notable event which affected the appearance of the downtown signscape was the modernize–Main Street movement. A campaign to modernize Main Street, promoted in architectural circles and abetted by store-front–replacement manufacturers, gained momentum in the 1930s. While store-front modernization had a long history prior to this movement, this campaign was particularly wide-ranging in scope, akin to an aesthetic movement. A rethinking of the nature of signs led to a closer integration of architecture and signage. Rather than applying a sign to a face of a building, as the Victorians had usually done, the modernists made the sign an inseparable part of the new façade.

The results, in many cases, were attractive new store-fronts which used signage as a major design element. The so-called art-deco store-

An appropriately tidy sign in Perth, Ontario, demonstrates that clarity is the key to a successful signboard.

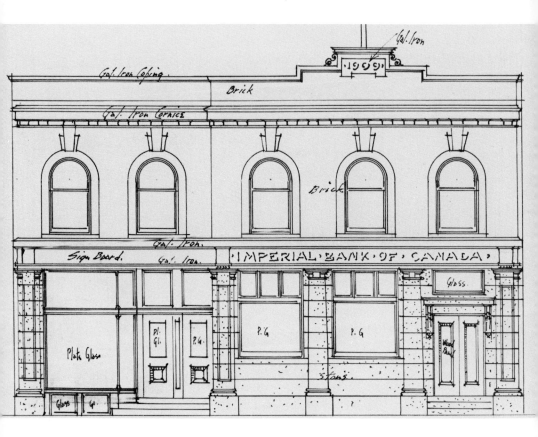

Plans for most older buildings allotted specific areas of the façade to appropriate signs, as did this 1909 design for a Moose Jaw business block.

fronts, now highly prized for their unique character, often depended on signage to create the design effect. Not only was the sign philosophically inseparable from the façade; it was often physically inseparable. Structural-glass store-fronts (using Carrara glass or Vitrolite) frequently carried the business name etched right into the glass with acid. This creates problems today when the business name changes, since replacement glass is no longer manufactured.

The third trend which had an influence on the image of downtown was the back-to-nature movement of the 1960s and 1970s, vestiges of which remain today. The nature movement, a general trend away from man-made or artificial products, particularly in the food industry, had a spin-off effect on many fields, including store-front design and the related sign industry. The result was a small but popular move to natural materials and handcrafting. This movement was closely associated with the environmental and preservation movements of the same period and was fuelled by the waves of nostalgia that swept the nation following the centennial (and the bicentennial in the United States). It also complemented the growing rejection of what was regarded as the sterility of the modern movement in architecture.

A corollary of this rejection was a token swing to preservation. The beauty of handcrafted workmanship was the supposed link between the preservation and the naturalist movements. Yet no attempt was made to assemble an academic basis for most of the work produced within the back-to-nature movement. A whole range of quasi-historical architectural elements was created, to be attached to any building and thereby to evoke the spirit of the old days. Some elements, like the omnipresent mock-colonial pediment, were intended to be imitative of a particular period in history. But hardware-store-colonial elements were rarely accurate in their design or appropriate in their placement. Signage too was colonialized, typically lettered in Old English script and hung from wrought-iron brackets projecting from the store-front.

The back-to-nature movement is more often associated with the later rustic mode. It was characterized by extensive use of bare, sandblasted bricks, cedar siding and shakes, and hand-carved or sandblasted signs. The art of the sign-maker made a come-back with this movement since a great deal of creative freedom was encouraged. In many ways this fascination with the rustic was as well suited to the reemergence of the handcrafted-sign industry as it was ill suited to the store-front–renovation industry. Whereas quite a few high-quality handcrafted signs, carefully designed to complement their buildings, were made and installed, very few store-front rustications were successfully wedded to older buildings.

An awning's end-panels can be used to advantage for signs.

OPPOSITE

A co-ordinated approach to window and hanging signs can be effective.

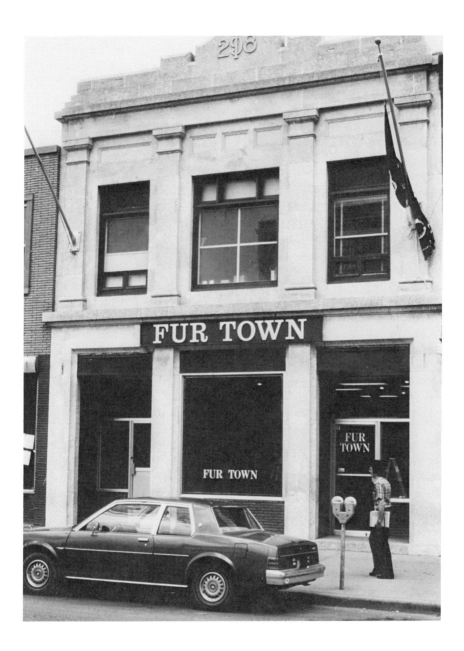

A move to new premises in Moose Jaw, Saskatchewan, spurred Fur Town to replace cramped and undistinguished signs (above left) with more appropriate signs, including a banner hung from an existing flagpole. Fur Town has a new image, and its reputation as the district's high-quality fur retailer has been reinforced.

The appropriateness of the changes in signage that resulted from the naturalist movement is relative. Assuming that the new sign does not detract from the basic architectural character of the building, and preferably complements it, then the sign should be considered suitable. Gross stylistic mismatches – such as a colonial hanging sign on an art-deco store-front – are obviously at odds and should be avoided.

The Legacy of Signage Today

Today our downtown signscapes are made up of the remnants of nineteenth- and twentieth-century signs and the layers of technologically 'improved' signs, including electrically lit versions. If we add to this the jumble of stylistic allusions developed to portray modern, progressive, historic-rustic, and other images fashionable at one time or another, we have the mixed legacy of our present downtown signscape. In order to come to grips with the difference between the nineteenth century's sign-dominated streetscape and today's much-maligned version, it is necessary to recognize the problems in our current streetscapes.

The problems with the downtown signscape began to mount at about the same time that sign-making ceased to be a local enterprise. Once the local craft became a regional industry, a local sign-maker's respect for the building, its context, and the local sign traditions were sacrificed for the benefits of mass production and big-city ideas. This may have opened the door to innovative ideas unfamiliar in many of our communities, but it also encouraged inappropriate signage downtown. This could occur in the form of signage designed for the highway, standardized signs placed on non-standard buildings, or any of a number of misconceived forms.

Recognizing the Problems

Understanding the problems of today's signscape is the first step towards developing appropriate solutions. Typical downtowns tend to suffer from certain common problems.

LEGIBILITY: The prime prerequisite of a good sign is that the message be clear and legible. A misguided attempt to use on a sign a typeface designed for the print media can render a sign virtually unreadable. The most common example of this misapplication is Old English script, a typeface best left to calligraphers and the printed page.

SCALE: A frequent problem is that the scale of signs does not relate to that of the buildings to which they are attached. A balance, where neither building nor sign dominates the other, is missing, to the detriment of the sign or, more often, the building.

NUMBER: There is a common approach to signage that sees security in numbers. The more signs there are, the more effective they are, goes the reasoning. Yet this is false security; a good deal of money is squandered on redundant signs, money which could have been more efficiently spent on one or two effective signs.

LAYERING: Signs conceived independently of their neighbours can create a discordant image downtown: a street rash of signs. The problem is self-perpetuating, as more signs are installed to out-shout their neighbours.

ORIENTATION: The automobile-oriented sign has been transplanted from the highway to downtown. These signs are designed to be read from great distances and by readers moving at high speeds, conditions that do not apply downtown, the traditional domain of pedestrians and slow-moving cars.

TARGET: Signage downtown is often poorly targeted or not targeted at all. A good sign must be designed and placed so that it is aimed at a specific target. A small projecting sign, for example, must not be placed so high as to escape the attention of its pedestrian target.

MASS PRODUCTION: Mass-produced signs, such as those standardized by soft-drink companies, tend to advertise a product rather than a business. Unless the business deals exclusively with that product, an inaccurate message about the business and product range will be presented to potential customers. Mass-produced signs also tend to be out of scale with the typical downtown building, often overwhelming the store.

Designing Appropriate New Signs

Redesigning an ineffective sign can be financially and aesthetically rewarding. An attractive sign can be a benefit rather than a neutral or even negative component for a business. Moreover, an entire downtown can benefit from the strength and visual appeal of a good signscape. A redesigned sign is no more than a reworking of the elements and tools formerly misapplied. The design process begins by establishing what image is intended, then works on developing ways to translate that intention into a built form, a sign. A logical starting place is with the range of sign types available. There are only four ways to affix a sign to a building:

SIGNBOARDS: A building's main business identification, signboards are flat, rectangular signs placed above the store-front. The message on a signboard is normally restricted to the name of the business, for the sake of clarity, but may include a very brief trade description. Sign-boards are targeted at the cross-street or automobile vantage point. In the same family but now generally out of favour are signs painted directly on to the building façade, generally on the upper storeys.

WINDOW SIGNS: These are painted on the inside of the main display windows. Traditionally, window signs were gold- or silver-leafed, but they are now more commonly painted. The message is kept brief, usually to the name of the business, and opaque backgrounds are avoided since they obscure the window display. Window signs are aimed at the pedestrian in the immediate vicinity or directly across the street.

PROJECTING OR HANGING SIGNS: Signs may be hung perpendicular to the building's face, often incorporating a logo or symbol. Indeed, some projecting signs were symbols only (a barber pole, for example). They are designed to be seen by pedestrians on the sidewalk adjacent to the building.

AWNING SIGNS: Some signs are painted directly on to the fabric face (rake), front edge (valance or flounce), or side panels of an awning or canopy. Many downtowns, for environmental reasons, have a tradition of extensive use of awnings. Awning signs can be targeted to any vantage point, depending on what part of the awning the name or the logo is painted.

Most older commercial buildings have a logical place for signage designed into the façade. It is usually most appropriate to take advantage of these locations when a new sign is being installed. Doing this capitalizes on both the local placement tradition and years of trial-and-error discovery of the most effective location. It is usually best to place a sign where it obviously belongs. Unfortunately, overlooking the obvious is not uncommon in the sign business. Sign placement should also respect neighbouring buildings and signs, but uniform sign placement down the street should not be imposed on non-uniform buildings. A variety of placements, each related to its own building, helps to counter a sterile signscape. Neighbourliness in sign appearance is a powerful tool for creating a dynamic yet cohesive visual image for downtown.

A carefully thought-out and designed typeface can clarify a sign and create a strong business image. Choosing an appropriate style of lettering or sign type can be as easy as looking at the business and the image it is projecting – or should be projecting. Classical typeface, cut into stone by banks in their turn-of-the-century temple buildings, helped to reinforce their image of stability and conservatism, and their signage, through the choice of typefaces and method of application, thus

Hooded lights, a happy marriage of traditional and contemporary design, and one of many alternatives to plastic-faced boxes

This striking art-deco building, clad in yellow and black Vitrolite and already a focal point of the street, was taken over by Ramsay's Photo and Art Supplies in Nelson, British Columbia, in 1982.

The new sign treatment developed for Ramsay's is evocative of the design era of the building and reinforces its strong visual impact on the street.

The standard internally lit, plastic-faced box sign can be as effective as other signs if due attention is given its design and placement. This matte-finished box has been designed to fit into the space framing the bay of a hotel tavern in Victoria.

mirrored their business or corporate image. The same principle can be
applied to any business. A conservative, progressive, avant-garde,
low-ticket, or high-ticket retailer's image can be reinforced by a typeface
which complements the image. A case in point is Fur Town, a business
in downtown Moose Jaw which was forced to move to new premises.
Here the business was presented with an opportunity to use signs to
reinforce its reputation as the district's high-quality fur retailer. The
original sign system – a back-lit plastic fascia sign, a projecting plastic
sign, and a plywood sign – was not indicative of the quality of the
business or its product. The new building (chosen partly for its classic
stone façade) also demanded better treatment than the run-of-the-mill
plastic sign. A sign system was developed which would complement
the triumvirate of quality: business, product, and building. Brass-faced
letters were chosen, brass being traditionally associated with quality;
maroon, a rich colour with royal connotations, was used as a background colour; and an easily read, classical typeface, Clarendon, was
chosen. Placed sensitively on the building, the sign reinforced all
aspects of the business image and became an additional merchandising
tool. The total cost of this owner-assembled sign in 1984 was $250.
Secondary signs complemented the package. An existing flagpole provided the opportunity to hang a banner at low cost, and window signs
were placed at pedestrian level. Both used the same style of type and
conveyed the same image of quality.

Another clue to choosing an appropriate typeface can be the building itself. With signage in a complementary typeface, an entire building
that is unique or visually notable in some way can become a de facto
sign. Ramsay's Photo and Art Supplies in Nelson, British Columbia, for
example, is a striking yellow and black art-deco building that was
already a focal point of the street. New signage was designed to harmonize with the style of the building and, as a result, now appears
integral to it. Historical photographs of a building can provide clues as to
the proper typeface to use to recreate a certain period ambiance.

Size, placement, and spacing of lettering on a sign are important for
legibility and readability. Legibility refers to the viewer's ability to
distinguish letters; readability refers to the reader's ability to grasp a
message. Both are determined by the nature of the lettering and how
the lettering is placed on the background. The minimum height of a letter
to be legible at thirty to fifty feet is one inch (different formulas produce different figures, so testing on site may be appropriate). In general,
the exclusive use of capital letters will result in a more easily read sign
than a mixture of capitals and lower-case letters. Words should be
spaced to be readable, with about 60 per cent of a signboard devoted to

lettering and the remainder to background. Highly decorative type-faces should be avoided, as should extra-bold or -fat styles; neither is particularly legible.

Other important considerations in sign design are contrast and colour. For signs on older downtown buildings, a compromise is in order. Although studies have shown that the contrast between yellow and black makes for the most legible sign, these colours are usually unsuited to older buildings. Less contrast is frequently in order lest the down-town begin to appear garish. Earth tones usually suit older masonry buildings, and lighter lettering on dark backgrounds can call attention to the message rather than the medium (this is particularly true of back-lit sign boxes). Limiting the sign's colour palette to two or at most three colours is a good rule of thumb. Too many colours can call attention away from the message.

Illumination should be considered if the business has significant after-dark sales. The notion of lighted twenty-four-hour signs is non-sense if everyone has a lighted sign. Lighted signs need not be limited to the standard internally lit, plastic-faced box. Alternatives may be more attractive, more effective, and more affordable. Traditional forms of lighted signs, notably neon, are effective. Direct illumination of a sign with hooded lights is another traditional form of lighting. Both of these methods are being used in contemporary architecture, enjoying a renaissance of sorts. As a result, they manage to convey both a tradi-tional and a modern image. Yet the plastic-faced box is a fact of life today. If a box is to be used, efforts should be made to fit it into the building, within the opening which frames the store-front, if possible. The background should be dark coloured and the lettering light, and the plastic face should have a matte finish to minimize the sheen.

The final factor determining choice of a sign is usually cost. But caution should be exercised; unlimited funds will not guarantee a good sign; and quality and expense are not synonymous. A budget should determine the type of materials used, not the quality. After all, a good sign should last years or decades with little maintenance. The use of inferior grades of materials not only shortens the life of a sign; it also creates image problems, as the materials weather poorly. The whole redesign rationale is short-circuited when second-rate materials or fabrication methods are used. A top-grade plywood is preferable to a bottom-grade oak. It is often less expensive, too.

The sign industry today is highly dependent on lease arrangements. Many large companies – and some small ones – will lease a sign to a business for a monthly rate which includes a maintenance agreement. This is attractive to the business person when the lease payments can

Well-intentioned by-laws regulating the size and placement of signs can be overly restrictive, taking some of the vitality out of the streetscape.

be claimed as a business write-off. Less frequently promoted, since it is less lucrative to the sign companies, is outright purchase of the signs. This option can be attractive to the independent merchant who would like to get out from under the never-own syndrome of lease. A sign that is not internally lit is virtually maintenance free and can be purchased for a few hundred dollars, or about three months of lease payments. Many business people find this option attractive.

Controlling Signs

Many cities and towns have attempted to inject order into the chaos of their downtown signage. There have been few uncompromised successes. This is not because order is difficult to achieve; rather, it is that order seems to drain the vitality out of the signscape. The problem is that the standard civic methods of creating order are not well suited to a highly personalized and creative beast like signage. By-laws, ordinances, and regulations were developed to protect the public health, welfare, and safety. When applied to signs, they were intended to secure the general safety of the public by setting minimum standards for electrical connections. Regulations concerning appearance normally dealt with aspects of signs which would confuse motorists, such as flashing or intermittent lights. A by-law or ordinance typically set out the minimum dimensions or conditions required to ensure compliance. In other words, virtually anything which met the minimum standards was considered acceptable (a number of cities also set selected maximum standards). This open-door approach to regulation has given us the best and the worst of our downtown signs.

More recently, the intent of ordinances and by-laws has been expanded to cover new ground. Included are protection of property values, creation of a more attractive economic and business climate, enhancement and protection of the physical appearance of downtown, and protection of the scenic and natural beauty of an area. Regulation mechanisms are stretched to the limit, however, when forced to encompass the diversified demands of appearance and property values. The regulations, designed to articulate size, set-back, projection, and illumination constraints, are not particularly suited to defining appropriateness and neighbourliness.

The regulatory approach does not promote good signage so much as it promotes non-offensive signage. It eliminates the most obnoxious signs, especially overpowering or street-dominating types. By the nature of by-laws and ordinances, definition is given to what is not allowed, not to what is encouraged. Formula solutions to design problems are easily developed from these documents, robbing the street of the vitality it likely once had. To some, the sterility of the over-regulated signscape is as unattractive as the clutter of the non-regulated street. Without due care, the creativity which enlivens the downtown can be stifled.

Encouraging Good Signs

Most downtowns do not have the good fortune to have a business community with a consensus of what constitutes good signage. Some direction and consistency is required. It is frequently up to an outside body to set the direction and arbitrate when necessary. The task is to encourage good signs and discourage bad ones. The trick is to do this without being able to quantify 'good' or 'bad' in a regulation.

One method that has had some measure of success in achieving this balance combines a limited by-law with a design-review board. The by-law provides full controls on public safety and limited controls on sign design, to eliminate gross offenders. Sign designs which pass the first screening are reviewed by a group of concerned people, who evaluate the appropriateness of the design. The review board (most often appointed by the city) is made up of citizens from a mixture of occupations, usually including a city-planning or community-development representative, an architect or professional designer, representatives of the downtown business community, and a citizen-at-large. The idea is to create a body of concerned and sensitive individuals who will gauge the tenor of downtown and determine whether a proposed sign will enhance the area. Some boards use guidelines to help members to develop a sensitivity to good design; others rely on instinct. Both can work. Accountability for decisions in either case rests with the board. For this reason, an appeal process is necessary.

A by-law and a design-review board will not eliminate all bad signs, but they can have a positive influence on good design and promote good signage downtown. As with other aspects of Main Street revitalization, gradual change, demonstrating by effective example rather than by imposition of a preconceived plan, creates a snowball effect whereby the broader potential of a district can gradually be realized.

Late-nineteenth-century infill construction in Quebec City

PETER HYNDMAN and GORDON FULTON

Sympathetic New Design

Even after old façades have emerged from behind aluminum siding and after new paint and new signs have been added, there is often room for improvement on Main Street. The streetscape might have some critical gaps that have come about through fire or the demolition of buildings. New infill building on such vacant lots has to be treated with special attention. The integration of brand-new construction, shaped by 1980s materials, building codes, and modest financing, presents the co-ordinator with some delicate issues. It would not be good policy to recruit a new merchant, attracted to town by the chance of establishing a business in a modern building, and then to put all sorts of obstacles in his way, particularly in the design field. This chapter will explore a variety of practical and hypothetical examples of new construction and infill buildings that respect the design approaches broached in the last two chapters. It will also address the related issue of adaptive reuse, whereby a building that is vacant can be refurbished rather than demolished, thus helping to maintain a degree of continuity in both streetscape and historical texture.

Sympathetic Infill

Vacant lots, or holes in the streetscape that have come about as the result of fire, neglect, or demolition, can become desirable sites for locating a new enterprise. A new building gives the Main Street co-ordinator an excellent opportunity to add to the visual and economic strength of the street. For all the historical detail present on Main Street, the economic realities of the contemporary marketplace may mean that a pragmatic approach must be taken towards new design. A museum-quality reconstruction, intended to be a facsimile of a since-demolished building or profusely decorated neighbour, is rarely feasible. Nor should it be a goal, for few streetscapes reflect a consistency of architecture from one period in time. More typically, the accumulation of buildings over many years, at slightly different heights and in different widths, styles, and materials, gives the contemporary Main Street a vitality which should be respected.

There are many approaches to the design of new buildings in an existing streetscape. A successful design – that is, a design which adds to the intrinsic character of the street – is possible with any of these approaches. Some, however, require a very high level of design skill and sophistication to be successful. Failure to come up with a building which 'fits' its context most often results from attempting a design approach without the required expertise at hand. Furthermore, each design problem is truly unique, and a solution which fits one location may be entirely wrong for another. There are no stock solutions for contextual architecture. There are a limited number of approaches, though, and finding the right approach can minimize the chances of creating a truly disastrous infill building.

The first of seven basic approaches to designing a building within an existing streetscape is an indifferent intervention. This approach is perhaps more correctly a lack of an approach, in that it does not respond in any way to the environment around the building. There is in the design no rapport, no exchange or sympathy with neighbouring buildings. The chances of pulling off a successful yet indifferent building are very remote. Unfortunately, a great deal of our downtown infill construction is indifferent at best.

The second approach is integration. Here an attempt is made to harmonize the design of a new building with those of adjacent buildings through the use of similar forms, sizes, details, materials, and colours. The range of possibilities of integration is quite wide, from a very close approximation of historical appearance to a simple acknowledgment of neighbouring colours and materials. The more successful designs produced by this approach tend to be consistent in intent, no matter how modest. For example, they do not mimic historical details, materials, and colours accurately while ignoring the building shape or size that accompanies that same model.

Integration was the approach taken in Bridgetown, Nova Scotia, when two new buildings were designed to fill a sizeable hole in the Queen Street streetscape. A fire in September 1982 had destroyed four

Three adjacent trust companies in downtown Victoria, British Columbia.
Montreal Trust's indifferent intervention ignores the existing streetscape.

Many small-town main streets have developed a gap-toothed appearance, often because of fire, as was the case on Queen Street in Bridgetown, Nova Scotia.

The infill solution chosen in Bridgetown was to integrate the new buildings with the old in a fairly literal translation of local historical precedents.

businesses and left six people homeless. Both of the pre-fire property owners expressed a willingness to rebuild on the site. The architect's preliminary design proposal for part of the site was based on the concept of integration – a two-storey block-and-wood-frame structure complete with parapet wall that almost matched the form and height of the previous structure. The building's form, size, details, materials, and colours were chosen to mimic local historical precedents in a reasonably literal fashion. The design proposal for the remainder of the site, however, lacked the consistency of the first building. The second building was to be of a different size and shape, with a facing material (antique brick) not part of the architectural vocabulary of the town. The Main Street co-ordinator helped to fine-tune the original design to make it consistent with the integration approach begun by its neighbour. The façade height was increased and the materials were changed in order to improve the second building's relationship to its context. Both buildings now contribute to the Bridgetown streetscape while meeting the needs and budgets of the owners.

A third approach, the antithesis of integration, is to contrast the new building with its neighbours. The general feeling in preservation circles is that contrast is not normally desirable, since it usually results in a building which has more visual impact than its neighbours. (Contrast can also, of course, produce a less outstanding building among buildings of visual bravura.) The assumption is that the existing streetscape has some intrinsic value which should not be upstaged by a new building. But clues to the way to use contrast effectively can be found in the architectural history of many small towns. Here, contrast was saved for buildings of some significance or importance: the city hall, the post office, the church, the bank, the provincial courthouse, or the land-titles office. Usually only one aspect was contrasted, such as scale or size, while others such as materials or window spacing were maintained. Even when the scale of a new building is vastly different from its surroundings, attempts can be made to relate it to its context in a systematic or controlled manner. Architect John M. Lyle, discussing his large-scaled Bank of Nova Scotia headquarters building across the street from historic Province House in Halifax (in the journal of the Royal Architectural Institute of Canada, January 1932), explained his controlled approach to contrast:

In designing the exterior we were anxious to strike a modern note but owing to the fact that the Parliament Building was just across the street we felt that certain characteristics of this very fine building should be echoed in the new building. So we developed the parti of recalling the channelled lower

Designed and built in the 1930s, the head office of the Bank of Nova Scotia in
Halifax contrasts dramatically with its historic neighbours in terms of scale,
yet by echoing their classic forms it has fit 'gracefully into its surroundings, as if
it had always been there.'

The proposed farmers'-market arch in Fort Macleod, Alberta: a 'precarious' or temporary structure affords an opportunity to experiment with local architectural forms.

*storey of the Parliament Building using a classic base on which to develop
our design, and by the use of Canadian forms endeavoured to strike a personal
note.*

Though the building dominated the downtown, the Halifax *Star* thought
it fit 'gracefully into its surroundings, as if it had always been there.'

A fourth approach to designing infill is sometimes called the 'precarious' approach. The intent is to create a temporary structure to house
an activity which may or may not continue once a permanent shelter is
created. A tent is an obvious example of a precarious building; while it
may do an admirable job of housing a farmers' market in the summer
(and be superior to a permanent building in many respects), it cannot be
considered a long-lasting addition to the streetscape. A building need
not be as obviously temporary as a tent to be precarious. Many towns
and cities have buildings dating from the Second World War that were
intended to provide temporary office space but have persisted to the
present day. There is a common folk belief that anything created as a temporary measure, especially by the government, will turn into a permanent addition. Since there is some truth to this, design of temporary or
precarious infill buildings should receive appropriate attention.

Precarious buildings may offer a designer the opportunity to have a
little fun with the local architectural vocabulary. There is a tendency
to be more accepting and receptive to variations on the local themes with
a structure which, in theory at least, is not to be a permanent addition
to the street. An entrance arch to a farmer's market proposed for downtown Fort Macleod has been designed in this spirit. The market has
been created in a vacant lot on Twenty-fourth Street, the town's main
street. The chances of constructing a new building on the site in the
short or medium term are not considered good by the townspeople, so a
'temporary' market entry has been proposed. It reflects some of the
characteristic shapes and proportions of downtown buildings but in a
much more playful, mannered, and exuberant fashion than might be
accepted in a permanent structure.

In recent years many architects have turned their attention to what
might be called the invisible approach to inserting new buildings into the
streetscape. The most characteristic form of 'invisible' building is the
mirrored-glass building, which, in theory, simply reflects its surroundings and makes little impact itself on the street. In concept this approach has merit, but in practical application it is rarely successful. It is
difficult to make a large entity such as a building simply disappear.
Most attempts to do this with mirrored glass become so striking in themselves that the result is a contrast of the highest order, since the forms,

The potential of architectural analogy – the reinterpretation of the past in a contemporary fashion – is effectively illustrated by this 1984 infill building in Quebec City. Old Quebec's characteristic forms provided the inspiration for this cheerful post-modern design.

OPPOSITE *top and bottom*

New infill buildings can be camouflaged. To maintain the historic appearance of Granville Street in Halifax, the new Barrington Place complex was almost completely hidden behind the Granville Street façades, which were disassembled during construction and then rebuilt in their original configurations.

The west side of Bridge Street in Sackville, New Brunswick, as it was in the mid-1960s. The Royal Bank of Canada occupied the columned brown sandstone building on the right, built in 1906.

OPPOSITE

top In 1974 the bank demolished the old branch and replaced it with a new building whose form, details, and materials are in stark contrast with the character and texture of the street.

bottom In response to citizen protest the bank reused a token bit of the old stonework in a wall beside the entrance, where it stands as an awkward and inadequate historical gesture.

size, details, materials, and colours of the new building are significantly different from those of its neighbours.

Other ways of making buildings invisible have been developed. Burying a building underground will remove its bulk from the landscape. A see-through or transparent building can minimize its impact on a street, but again, such a building may contrast very strongly with its neighbours. In the right circumstances a new building can be camouflaged. In a more rural setting, vegetation can minimize the visual impact of a building by blurring the edges between it and its surroundings. In an urban setting, hiding a new building behind another building or façade can make it invisible from the normal viewing angles of the street. A great deal of controversy exists in the preservation field about so-called façadism – grafting an historical façade on to a new building as a gesture to preservation. As with all the approaches outlined here, it is both the skill and the appropriateness of such an action which determine the success of the finished product. There are appropriate places for façadism and appropriate places for total building preservation. A successful façade-transplant was completed on Granville Street in Halifax, where the overriding preservation goal was to maintain the exterior appearance of the streetscape, which fronted the new Barrington Place.

The 'analogous' approach to new buildings recreates certain aspects of the surrounding environment while introducing a modern touch elsewhere in the building. A strong desire for continuity combined with a perhaps equally strong desire for difference characterizes this analogy of integration. The danger of this design approach is that it may result in a schizophrenic building which is neither old nor new, fish nor fowl. Yet a well-designed analogous building which reinterprets the past in a contemporary fashion may capitalize on the best each era has to offer. The differentiation may be at the level of architectural detail or at the level of the general form of the building. As with the integration approach to new construction, there is a wide range of options available for designing an analogous building; in fact, the analogous approach can be seen as a continuation of the integration approach, with design solutions that drift further and further from approximating an historical façade.

The last of the basic approaches to designing a building within an existing streetscape is to combine several of the previous approaches at the same time. This too must be done in a deliberate and conscientious manner if it is to be successful. This complex approach – the complexity residing in the designer's attitude, that is, not necessarily in the project – is an attempt to satisfy a number of potentially conflicting design requirements: to integrate and contrast at the same time; to make both

The Cambridge Arts Centre found a new home by adapting a 'theatre' of a different sort – a church – into a performing-arts centre. Though now closed, the old entrance still commands attention on Water Street; the new entrance, tucked around the side of the centre, lacks the street presence of the original.

modern and historical references; to camouflage while making a visual statement. It may be possible to break a project down into its diverse components and apply the appropriate design approach to each component in turn while not sacrificing the overall unity of the project. But this is not easy to accomplish. The danger is that a focus and a strong sense of design intent can be lost.

Such a design issue arose in Sackville, New Brunswick. There the Royal Bank had occupied a stalwart structure built in 1906 in the heart of the town's imposing red-sandstone commercial district. The bank decided that the old branch was no longer functional. It pointed to a columned interior space that was laid out poorly for efficient banking and could not be redesigned well, to exterior stairs that were allegedly dangerous for elderly people as well as invalids, to roof trusses that had weakened, and to exterior columns that were suffering from internal rot. The bank conducted feasibility studies to see whether it could rehabilitate the building but concluded that it could not do so to satisfy its own business needs and comply with the National Building Code. The bank considered giving the building to the town for use as a library, but because of its prime location at the intersection of Main and Bridge streets, it decided to rebuild on the site.

The Royal Bank's Montreal architects produced a design for a new branch, and in 1974 demolition work began. Despite local protest, a senior bank official claimed that the old building had no appreciable merit and needed replacement. The new design was approached as a contrast to the historical streetscape, with the form, details, and materials of the new building at odds with its sandstone neighbours. Local citizens felt that this approach was inappropriate and insensitive, so the bank produced a compromise scheme. This approach was a complex of contrast, analogy, and façadism that attempted to be modern while at the same time making an historical gesture by incorporating a token part of the stonework from the old building in a wall beside the main entrance. The issue had been missed. In local opinion the approach was wrong, not the details of the design (though there was also serious concern about the quality of the design, which compounded the problem). The new building provides more efficient facilities for customers and staff and is successful on that level, but it is unsuccessful as an appropriate design solution to the larger problem of urban infill design.

A word of caution is in order here concerning the importance of consulting design professionals. It is doubtful that a Main Street co-ordinator will control the complete design process of a building. This may be due to time constraints or to simple inability to do so. While some co-ordinators have design backgrounds, many others come from the dis-

The old Carnegie library in Perth, Ontario, an abandoned hulk after a devastating fire, was sensitively rehabilitated and given a reprieve. It now houses prestige office space.

The old Capitol Theatre in Moose Jaw, Saskatchewan, a Main Street landmark, was declared functionally obsolete – too big, too costly to operate – and closed by Famous Players in 1982. An independent firm, Mayco, carefully reworked the interior, dividing it into three smaller theatres without sacrificing its architectural character. It is now a successful triplex.

ciplines of planning and commerce. The practice of architecture is governed
by provincial associations of architects, which have regulations that
must be followed. If there is any question about the amount of design work that may be done by a co-ordinator, it would be advisable
to check with the local association to find out what one can and
cannot do; best of all, know when to get assistance from a registered
architect.

That proviso aside, a co-ordinator can play a critical role in settling
design issues. In addition to helping to check codes and regulations, a
co-ordinator may be involved in some sort of design-review committee.
This body can act as a heritage watch-dog and require an appropriate
design approach as a condition of design approval. Not all provinces
make the approval of design-review boards mandatory, but Nova
Scotia, for example, includes it in the approval stage of applications for
capital funds towards Main Street revitalization. Any potential re-
cipient of such provincial funds must complete a form for a design-
review committee, describing such details as materials, height, colours,
and relationship to surrounding buildings. Assisting an architect and his
client at this stage can start the design process in the right direction. A
design-review committee is typically composed of a design professional
(often an architect), a member of the provincial department concerned
with fund allocation (if applicable), members of the business community,
and a citizen- or citizens-at-large. Even if the committee does not have
the legal clout to enforce its recommendations, the peer pressure in a
small town can often have the same effect as a legally binding recom-
mendation. The key is to involve the business community to the fullest
extent possible and to charge them with setting a mutually agreeable
design direction for the downtown. A co-ordinator can help to pass on
an understanding of the principles of appropriate design to other
members of the design-review committee in order to ensure that the
process of sympathetic revitalization continues after he or she leaves.

Adaptive Re-use

Most communities have a white elephant or two near their main streets.
Studies have shown that it is often cheaper to rehabilitate a structure
than to tear it down and build from scratch. A structure that seems out of
date and ugly to one generation may become a heritage gem to another.
Garages built in the 1950s, a 1930s theatre, and a host of old churches or
other religious structures have proved themselves adaptable to other
uses. As a result of the 1925 union of the Presbyterian and Methodist
churches, Bridgetown had a spare church. This became the home of

the Rothsay Masonic Lodge, a group that could use the interior space of the church. In Cambridge, Ontario, the First Baptist Church has become a theatre, another use where an original design feature – the pulpit, now a stage – could be exploited. The transformation took place with significant input of civic funds, as well as grants from the Ontario Heritage Foundation and Wintario. The former Galt Little Theatre became the Cambridge Arts Centre, with the Galt group as the prime tenant. The facility can be used by other community groups. In this case, however, there have been some drastic alterations to the exterior façade. The front door has been blocked in and the main entrance moved off to one side. While this may be better for circulation and fire codes, it is surprising that the old front door was not capitalized upon for its eye-catching quality – perhaps at least as a focus for advertising information. Such an aesthetic response certainly raises the question of how much structural alteration can be tolerated before a building loses its architectural integrity.

Sometimes the adaptive reuse goes hand in hand with retail recruitment. Bridgetown, situated along a major tourist route through the Annapolis Valley, could usefully add a restaurant. Where could this go? One solution would be to modify one of the splendid old houses of the town, as has been done in the case of Wolfville's Blomidin Inn or Sackville's Marshlands Inn. Another would be to convert an abandoned gas station that lies half-way down Queen Street at an important intersection. Sketches for exploiting the open space under the canopy, and perhaps for forecourt seating, show that the building modification could be simply done. Folding french windows would permit a flexible response to weather. Alternatively, the site could become the location of a fresh-fruit and -vegetable market. The service bays would provide good storage, and the forecourt ample space for summertime display.

Institutional buildings often provide a ready-made heritage setting for new offices or restaurants. The present town hall in Bridgetown was originally the post office, built in the 1920s. A decision was made to relocate the post office in the 1960s, and, thanks to the insistence and persuasion of a former town councillor, this building – with its location at the top of the T intersection – now provides the town offices with a prime location and good, usable office space. In Cambridge, the old post office, built in 1904, has been turned into the Old Post Office Restaurant. The high ceilings and interior trim have been exploited as an elegant surrounding for dining, while an addition to the rear, overlooking the Grand River, provides additional lounge and dancing space. In Perth, a fire in the old Carnegie library provided an

opportunity for rehabilitation into office space for the real-estate firm
of Crane and Schooley. In Moose Jaw, the old post office, built in 1911,
was adapted as the city hall in 1963 – an early example of the city's
commitment to reusing its architectural assets. Recently the old Capitol
Theatre, another gem on Moose Jaw's Main Street, was saved, its
interior sensitively rehabilitated as a triplex cinema. A greater variety of
films can be shown at the same time; turnover will be more vigorous,
and the community gained a significant addition to its cultural facilities.

An evolving design philosophy, supported by an informed design-
review committee and media, can introduce respectful design into
the midst of the most disparate of structures. Property owners and
merchants, designers and citizens can all be convinced, by cumulative
example, that good design and good business are compatible.

A merchant in Nelson, British Columbia, attends to details
before his doors are open.

CHRIS PELHAM and DON MACINTOSH

Taking Care of Business

It is not enough that a shop have a renovated façade, or a fresh coat of paint, or an eye-catching sign. All this would amount to little if the shop did not have proper window displays and its street the right retail mix. An effective shop produces window displays that draw customers inside. That is what happened when Shaw's of Perth hired a window-display artist one Christmas. Articles sold so well from the window that it had to be redone three times during that pre-Christmas season.

Windows are a retailer's number-one source of inexpensive advertising. Good display windows help to establish a store's presence and its image of style and quality. They introduce the retailer to the consumer. The window is the store's face; it gives the customer an all-important first impression. Window displays should be clear and concise. They should attract their audience, create an image through quality and quantity of merchandise displayed. Timing is important. Seasonal specials should be promoted, or sales on surplus merchandise. If a heat wave is expected, air-conditioners could be displayed, or coolers, tents, and cotton outfits. It is an even better idea to promote seasonal specials in a co-ordinated way through a merchant group. Common themes such as heritage days, fall harvest, Santa's village, or the twelve days of Christmas can focus promotion effectively. Through co-ordinated presentations every window display reinforces those of its neighbours. Together they attract business from outside the community as well as from within.

There are many questions which must be asked about a window display. Is it too crowded? Too empty? Is there a focal point? Are the

props effective? What would happen if fluorescent lighting were replaced by warmer incandescent spotlights? Would an awning help to
cut down glare and protect the colour of the merchandise on display?
Could the mannequins benefit from new wigs? Does the odd finger or
two need repair?

The window is vital as a sales-promotion tool. A window reaches
customers who did not see the newspaper advertisements. It should
also duplicate the presentation of merchandise featured in those advertisements. Both the window display and newspaper advertising sell
merchandise directly and build a reputation for the store, but a
window display has advantages over the newspaper as an advertising
medium: it is used at the point of purchase (a customer who looks at
merchandise in the window is only a dozen steps away from buying it); it
can employ natural colour to its full effectiveness, while a newspaper
usually uses black and white photos or drawings; and it presents the
merchandise itself, life-size. It is important to change a window frequently. This helps to keep displays timely. It also familiarizes the
customer with a wide variety of merchandise. Frequent window changes
also protect merchandise from sun fading, dust, and dirt. One useful
encouragement for such a turnover is to organize a display-of-the-month
competition. The prize might be only a small plaque placed in the
window and donated by some group in the community. Sometimes a
bank can be persuaded to sponsor such an exercise, or perhaps a
combination of downtown merchants can be the sponsors.

Descriptive signs in the window make the selling more emphatic.
Professionally lettered signs are not achieved with magic markers unless
the writer has training in lettering. Dry-transfer lettering (Letraset,
Geotype) on a piece of stiff artboard is far more effective. It is usually
wise to keep copy to a minimum; otherwise, it may detract from the
rest of the display. The converse can be true, however, when it comes to
sale signs. Sale signs often spell out the benefits of purchasing a
particular item, or compare sale price to regular price as an inducement
to the customer; that is, they outline what is special about the sale
item.

Retail Mix

While improvements can be made to a store through attention to its
window display, the broader display of the Main Street community
may also need treatment. The shopping centre or mall is one of the
reasons for the current demise of Main Street. While the architectural
and social ambiance of the mall is not something that Main Street needs

The reflection of the farmers' market in Cambridge, Ontario, can be seen in the windows of this West Indian specialty store.

to emulate, the mall's approach to marketing and sales offers pointers for revitalized downtown-merchant groups. Shopping centres were created to meet a set of marketing projections based on statistics and surveys which show a return of profits to their investors. Shopping centres are an expensive proposition to build. To protect this investment, managers are assigned to each centre. The manager who runs a shopping centre constantly reviews its monthly performance statistics against a performance model. Each tenant is reviewed monthly by his gross sales per square foot. Those tenants who perform well are encouraged and rewarded. Those tenants who do not measure up are informed of their performance and subject to being replaced.

A mall manager constantly searches for prospective tenants to improve the mall's performance statistics. The manager knows what his retail mix is, what it should be, and what sorts of commercial spaces are available and when. He should know, by his monthly projections, what his costs will be for promotion, upkeep, and utilities; this allows him to be specific when dealing with prospective tenants or talking to his leasing department. The manager's goal is to run his shopping centre as efficiently as possible and return as large a profit as possible.

A downtown can monitor its performance in a similar manner. It can fill its vacant stores to increase its own mix of shops and businesses. Shopping centres have their management companies; downtowns should have business organizations with functions and responsibilities of the same type. In many cases these organizations – business-improvement associations, districts, and the like – already exist. Downtown is unlikely to be managed just as a mall is because individual merchants do not all sign a lease with one organization and individual monthly statistics are not generally available. Individual merchants want to retain their autonomy. However, on behalf of the merchants a co-ordinator can assemble a profile of the downtown and available commercial space to help to improve the retail mix. It is important to have the profiles current and available to potential downtown investors. The co-ordinator can assist the existing organization by offering technical and advisory services. Often, it is just an initial spurt of energy that is needed; then the business community itself can build a self-sustaining management. In Windsor, Nova Scotia, for example, support for the Business Improvement Development Commission was slow to build, but once the merchants realized the potential benefits of such an organization, they became supportive. Efforts to co-ordinate lighting displays at Christmas, to set up meetings to discuss promotions, and to develop a policy on a variety of planning initiatives received a positive response.

Business-improvement associations should have committees which address particular areas of a business community's concern. One committee should deal with retail recruitment, searching out new tenants. A representative from the local council or municipal staff would be a useful member of a search committee because the search usually requires assistance from both private and public sectors. In this way a community can encourage private reinvestment and demonstrate public commitment to its own downtown. While each business-improvement association will have a natural bias in favour of its own community, it should review its assets and liabilities objectively. Public amenities, parking and public transportation, population, and industrial and commercial opportunities should all be surveyed. A critical tour of neighbouring communities should also be considered, for with comparative data the tenant-search committee is more able to highlight the benefits of its community to a prospective retailer or business.

The tenant-search committee should prepare a quantitative analysis which outlines the state of the community. The chamber of commerce, the local real-estate board, and municipal staff can assist here. A file on vacant downtown buildings, one that includes a profile of each building, should be prepared. Consideration should be given to date and type of construction, size, amenities and facilities, zoning, parking availability, occupancy, available space, rent, rates and taxes, selling price, leasing conditions, and contact person. A sense of how neighbouring communities match up to this profile is useful. The co-ordinator can help here by conducting a survey on market size and market need, so that prospective merchants – and the existing group – can understand their zones of influence.

Market Determination

There are many professional theories on market determination and scores of consultants who are able to carry out proper market definition and analysis. If financial resources permit, the services of even a part-time consultant would be a wise investment. One of the first things a co-ordinator should do is undertake a market analysis. Market analysis and retail recruitment are ongoing projects for a co-ordinator and typically begin with the definition of a geographic area from which customers might reasonably be drawn. The distances customers will commute will depend on the length and convenience of the trip. Highway quality, transit services, and natural barriers all play a part. A consumer twenty miles away on good highways may be more likely to shop downtown than one five miles away by indirect and inconvenient access. Newspaper-distribution statistics are sometimes helpful in

Learning to dress a mannequin, at the Main Street window-dressing seminar in Perth, Ontario

developing a profile of a community's hinterland. A graphic representation of the geographical boundaries of a market often takes the form of a map with concentric circles representing five, ten, fifteen, and more miles' distance from downtown, calibrated against time and convenience.

A profile of the characteristics of the people living within the geographic trading area can be developed with the assistance of Statistics Canada, Canada Post, and local planning and assessment departments. Such considerations as age, sex, family size, average family income, and number of dwelling units are basic items of information in the profile. Especially important are male-to-female ratios and age distribution. From this data, simple mathematical computation will reveal the number of potential customers for a children's clothing store, for example, or a ladies'-wear fashion shop catering to the fifty-and-over age bracket. This number of potential customers can be compared to known threshold numbers for certain operations, published in retailing guides. Areas of surplus and deficiencies for a given community can then be quickly outlined.

Yet such statistics are virtually meaningless unless the existence of the potential market is confirmed or defined by popular opinion. To back up the statistical probability of a given market, a consumer survey is often conducted. Telephone surveys, structured to obtain information relevant to a small-town situation, can be used to gauge popular opinion. In Windsor, Nova Scotia, for example, in order to determine the validity of the conclusions reached about its 25,852-person market, an extensive (approximately 15 per cent) telephone consumer survey was conducted. Organized by Nova Scotia's Department of Municipal Affairs, the survey was structured to obtain information relevant to the local situation. The market was segmented geographically. Each region was polled, tabulated, and analysed individually. The results were predictable in some cases and startling in others: only one-half of the 25,852 market habitually shopped in Windsor. Although current and future efforts will yield a higher proportion, today's reality is that Windsor's actual market is somewhat fewer than 13,000 persons.

From the investor's point of view, locating a store is a two-phase process. First he must select a community. A good community is characterized by economic growth and overall stability, a good trading area, not too much competition in his field, compatibility with the merchant's personality, and political co-operation. Secondly, he must select a site. A good site is characterized by appropriate traffic flow and accessibility, location of both competing and supporting stores, and quality of local building codes and by-laws. A pro forma income statement, calculating anticipated sales and expected expenses (rent, salaries,

Quality merchandise was being presented in a confused manner in this window in Perth, Ontario (top). By experimenting with contemporary display techniques (bottom), the proprietors learned how to transform the window into a model of effective merchandising.

The proprietor of Moose Jaw's Main Street Gun Shop poses proudly during World Curling Week with her prize-winning window display.

taxes, advertising, and so on), gives an investor a sense of potential profit.

Retail Recruitment

With all the relevant information in hand – including a market analysis – a plan should be developed by the tenant-search committee that determines the existing growth potential and the preferred retail mix. It should set reasonable objectives – it is unlikely, for instance, that Eaton's can be lured to a very small city or town. Based on the available space and the missing retail operations required for the preferred retail mix, specific types of desirable retail operations can be determined. Once these retail types have been identified, then the tenant-search committee can identify retailers who might want to come to the community. There is no magic to recruitment: it demands commitment and long hours. It is not just a nine-to-five job. It requires constant review. Tenants are brought into a community; they rarely walk in unassisted.

A community's best source of potential new retailers is the pool of existing merchants: those who wish to relocate, expand, or diversify, or those who know someone who wants to open a store. The tenant-search committee should talk with businesses and their financial institutions and present its community analysis to them. It must be remembered that small, independent retailers are normally the key to success in smaller downtowns, and efforts should be made to appeal to these business people as well as to the larger national chains. Since many commercial leasing brokers do not want to bother with the smaller retailer, this gives an opportunity to the tenant-search committee.

To maximize the chances for success in downtown retail recruitment, six basic points should be kept in mind.

1 Begin at once and close to home. Contact every merchant who can be considered a good addition for downtown. Most small-store leases are obtained by direct personal contact.
2 Survey all existing businesses for expansion or relocation needs that can be satisfied within the downtown. This can free up space that is better suited for different types of retailing.
3 Survey local suppliers, wholesalers, co-operatives, and franchise organizations for prospective new tenants. Keep in touch, and provide current, usable information.
4 Follow and verify every lead with a professional team of merchants, bankers, realtors, and city officials.
5 Know your market potential; know where there are gaps in goods and

services; decide which types of businesses are best, and go after them.
6 Repeat the whole process again and again.

Downtown improvement encompasses far more than changes to façades, signs, or street furniture. It also requires the efficient selling of goods and providing of services. Without such economic activity, any architectural preservation or public improvements will soon deteriorate due to lack of care or maintenance. There is an impressive set of resources available to the business community. Reports can be obtained from the major chartered banks – financial analyses of trends in wholesaling and transportation, pamphlets on stock inventory and flow, and the like. The Federal Business Development Bank offers advice and seminars, and associations of independent retailers provide regional and national umbrellas for local activities. All in all, the resources are there with which the merchant community may be reinvigorated. The merchants deserve attention, since in many communities they are among the leading employers. While the mall and shopping centre have lured away many consumers through their advantages of choice and variety, Main Street can, if it organizes properly, offer the same vigorous variety – with the bonus of delight that comes from making these transactions in a community-oriented environment.

The first Old Home Week in Perth, Ontario, 1905

JIM MOUNTAIN

Promoting and Marketing Downtown

Consumers today are far more mobile than they were when most of Canada's main streets were established. In the West it is not uncommon for people to travel more than a hundred kilometres to work, shop at a large urban centre, or go out for the evening. At the other end of the country, 51 per cent of the labour force of Windsor, Nova Scotia, work in Halifax, sixty-six kilometres away, and 26 per cent shop there once a week. Many small towns have powerful competitors nearby. Shoppers in Cambridge, Ontario, are an hour away from metropolitan Toronto; shoppers in Perth, an hour away from Ottawa. Regional shopping malls, located on the outskirts of a built-up area or at some freeway or highway set between several smaller communities, are another problem. Small downtowns frequently watch regional malls drain away their potential customers. How can small downtowns compete with their larger metropolitan neighbours? What strategies can be devised to strengthen the hearts of these towns? A key element in the renewal of economic and social activity downtown is innovative promotion.

People often visit another town or city because it has been promoted as having an exciting variety of services, stores, or restaurants. For communities close to major metropolitan areas this is especially a problem. Sometimes the old home-town is viewed as a place to escape from, and this, too, helps to strengthen the magnet of other, larger communities. In Fort Macleod, Alberta, for example, a 1981 survey by the University of Lethbridge School of Management Studies found that consumers annually purchased 60 per cent of their furniture and

In Nelson, British Columbia, opportunities to promote the community are seldom overlooked. Many civic events are now arranged to coincide with the visits of campaigning politicians. Here the Honourable Flora MacDonald places a plaque on a street planter.

appliances, 40 per cent of their clothing, 45 per cent of their food, and 80 per cent of their entertainment in the city of Lethbridge, a thirty-minute drive away. For Windsor, Nova Scotia, slightly more than 10 per cent of the town's consumers did their food shopping in New Minas and bought almost 10 per cent of their furniture in Halifax. This pattern exists for many towns across Canada and is likely to persist. And yet if a town can keep its residents at home some 10 to 15 per cent longer during their leisure and shopping time, a corresponding number of consumer dollars will stay in that community. Even small communities have been able to lure away customers from their larger neighbours by highlighting the unique, special, or exciting things about their towns.

It is essential that small towns be competitive with their neighbours. One role of the downtown co-ordinator is to get all of the town's interest groups to work together to promote a positive image of themselves to local residents and to the surrounding region. A community's vitality could hinge on the level of energy devoted to organizing and promoting itself. Here are some of the techniques that have worked.

A Town's Assets

Many of the promotional events will involve the downtown merchants, so the first group to contact is the business-improvement organization, board of trade, or chamber of commerce. The promotional co-ordinator should have a list of all the relevant contacts. Equally important is the compilation of a volunteer registry. Community volunteers give invaluable help in the promotion of special events, which, characteristically, are labour intensive. Officials within the town's municipal government system are also important. A co-ordinator should know what each department's responsibilities are and begin to cultivate the support of town employees. This includes the street and traffic workers, those in the shop, town office staff, the town clerk (or secretary-treasurer), and the town manager. The co-ordinator should learn the procedures and by-laws affecting permit approvals: most outdoor events, for example, require approval by municipal authorities. He should also establish a rapport with the local health inspector. There are very strict rules governing the sale of dairy products, meat, or eggs; failure to comply with these could quickly shut down a farmer's market. Local by-laws should be checked. Plans for site delineation, parking, traffic, and crowd control should be discussed fully with the fire and police departments.

The co-ordinator should keep a record of the meeting dates of key municipal committees. Most meetings are bi-weekly or monthly, so

The Fort Macleod, Alberta, powwow was traditionally held on the grounds of city hall.

Revived in 1983, the powwow has again become an annual event.

planning should begin well ahead. Town politicians and community leaders must be kept informed of the progress of projects and, whenever possible, involved in actual events. Store openings, festivals, various commemorative ceremonies, and parades are the types of events that build a positive image for the town. It is a good idea to invite the area's provincial or federal representatives to the most significant activities. Do not overextend the relationship, however, by requesting their presence at every event.

Both the federal and provincial governments can provide useful assistance for special events. At the federal level, the Secretary of State's office provides Canada Day grants to assist local festivals. Provincial holidays also sometimes have grant programs. Alberta's Heritage Day grant helped sponsor a powwow and Old West festival in Fort Macleod on the long weekend of August 1983. This event revived a long-standing activity and attracted some twelve hundred people, locals and tourists, most of whom had not seen the like before. For an event such as this, which could capitalize on Fort Macleod's proximity to the Blood Reserve, Indian dancers and five drum groups travelled considerable distance to attend. It is a long-standing tradition that such revered dancers and drummers are paid to perform, and so a significant portion of the two-thousand-dollar grant helped to support their presence at the powwow. Portions of the funds were also used to provide a puppet show, materials for face-painting, to subsidize a barbeque beef-on-a-bun picnic for 250 people, to stage an outdoor band concert, and to rent a sound system for the day. Nearly every community in Canada is familiar with such traditional activities. These can be used by the downtown community to promote itself, either as a once-a-year activity or as a continuing series of events.

Branches of federal and provincial governments responsible for employment can also be useful sources of funds. Employment and Immigration Canada, through its Canada Employment centres, administers a number of employment programs which can provide staff for projects related to downtown revitalization. These programs tend to vary by the year or the season and in recent years have appeared under names such as NEED, Canada Works, or LEAD. These may be sponsored by municipalities or, in some cases, by non-profit organizations. The local Canada Employment centre should be contacted for information regarding government-funded job opportunities. Even if this is for clean-up work – for example, on a site that is in the vicinity of downtown but deemed unsuitable or unsavoury – such a project could become an asset to the community and to related promotions. A good example from the Heritage Canada project towns is found in Windsor, Nova Scotia, where

The dock and boat-launching wharf in Windsor, Nova Scotia

West Coast fish for sale at the farmers' market in Fort Macleod, Alberta

The local RCAF detachment on parade in Fort Macleod in the late 1940s

Touring politicians regularly delivered addresses from this bandstand in Fort Macleod. Now refurbished, the structure once again hosts many civic activities.

a park and wharf were provided for Pisiquid Lake. This body of water, formed when a new highway cut across to Falmouth and for many years hardly used, became a place enjoyed by recreational sailors, canoeists, and swimmers. The park adjacent to the wharf was sodded, a bandstand erected, and trees planted. Entry to the park is by a new parking lot, which also serves the business community along Water Street. Since Water Street used to be the centre of the nineteenth-century port town, this construction reinforces other heritage initiatives that had begun on various town buildings.

It has been estimated that the federal grants which helped to develop this park amounted to $71,000 and employed nine men over seven months. That activity in turn has generated a recent $500,000 grant from the province of Nova Scotia for the redevelopment of Windsor's waterfront. The money will be spent on three related activities: the improvement of the active recreation area; creation of a land mass for private-sector commercial development; and a passive recreation corridor, for sitting and watching. A bike path is also planned. Windsor's attractiveness as a multiple destination – for shopping, business, and recreation – will be enhanced by what began as a make-work project. Provincial government departments responsible for job creation also sponsor a variety of similar programs. Alberta's Student Temporary Employment Program enabled nine students to be hired for a summer-theatre project in 1983 and provided a tourist-oriented use for the old Empress Theatre in Fort Macleod. Alberta Agriculture is encouraging local farmers' markets, and in 1983 there were one hundred across the province receiving its support. For that to happen a community has to organize two markets by itself. Fort Macleod's attracted only three sellers at first; later, the number climbed to eight. These included farmers from neighbouring Hutterite colonies, Japanese Canadian market gardeners from two hundred kilometres away, a person who had come all the way from the West Coast to sell fish, a honey stall, and a local artist selling various handcrafted items. Downtown merchants took advantage of this event to put their own tables in front of their stores.

Potential activity sites can be identified through an inventory of a town's physical resources. The co-ordinator should tailor the activity to the capability of the sponsoring organization. He should also be practical about such considerations as the effect of weather on the site, parking and traffic flow, accessibility for the impulse spectator, and availability of washrooms, water, and electrical sources.

The street itself, Main Street, is often the community's richest physical resource. A good way to begin assessing its potential is to do archival work, both in the local newspaper records and in the regional museum's

A once little-used cinema in Fort Macleod now hosts popular day- and night-time theatre.

below
A valentine-card contest hosted by the Main Street office in Fort Macleod

photo collection. What were the traditional parade routes? Why were
they there? After the Main Street office organized the first Santa Claus
parade in Fort Macleod, we were told by a long-time resident that it had
been the first time in eighty-five years that a parade had taken that
direction. In Fort Macleod there is nearly always a very strong wind
blowing from the opposite direction. Luckily, it had been a calm day, for
weather can be a big factor; horses hate going into the wind and it
would not have made for a calm parade if the wind had been strong. Old
photos can also suggest where some of the traditional meeting sites
have been and what kinds of activities have been held there in the past.
Fort Macleod's town square had held chautauquas, markets, pow-
wows, and cricket games. Copies of such historical images can be added
to promotional literature that is distributed beyond the town, or added
to window displays during the week leading up to the event.

An outdoor bandstand is an asset to a town and is nearly always
under-utilized. Fort Macleod's had been used by Prime Minister Wilfrid
Laurier in the election of 1911 but had been unused since 1951. A local
citizen's group salvaged it in the mid-1970s and placed it on a concrete
base. It has recently been given a coat of paint, and its hedge has
been trimmed and thinned. The downtown bandstand is now used for
children's events, music workshops, and the Heritage Day festival.

A theatre is another natural facility for attracting people downtown if
it can offer programs of interest to the community. Effective management of a small-town theatre by a private owner or non-profit organization requires time, effort, and expertise. If developed properly, local
theatre can produce benefits for adjacent businesses, for a town's tourist
trade, and for community cultural life. Other useful downtown facilities
include senior-citizen's centres, museums, walkways, vacant lots, and
town-office or courthouse properties. Vacant buildings can be rented for
one-shot special uses – as, for instance, Santa's headquarters at
Christmas. It is important that activities be as close as possible to the
downtown core. The spin-off effects both for business and for the
downtown's image provide convincing arguments to bring before town
officials and business owners.

Planning

When an inventory of a town's resources is complete, a promotional
program should be planned and a realistic set of goals determined. Improving downtown's image, increasing retail sales, and encouraging
special events, cultural activities, tourism, and new shops will be
among a town's general aims. A series of promotions for the entire year

should be planned. There are three types of promotions: retail sales, special events, and general promotional programs.

Retail sales are mainly commercial in nature. They include sidewalk sales, $1.49 days, or are geared to occasions such as Mother's Day, harvest season, or back-to-school time. It is possible to generate extra interest in these sales by turning them into mini special events, planning fun activities such as a Valentine-card contest, Easter sale, or Hallowe'en haunted house to coincide with them. Special events such as theme parades and festivals require more planning, bigger budgets, and considerably more work. Most communities have traditional events which can be integrated into the downtown-revitalization project. Perth, Ontario, has its Festival of the Maples, while Moose Jaw has a day-long parade every spring in which marching bands from all over North America join Canadian bands to parade through the wide Main Street. Windsor, Nova Scotia, has its Sam Slick Days, capitalizing on the image of the region's most famous literary character. Special events can involve months of planning by a co-ordinating committee. Publicity for these events should begin three weeks before the scheduled date. If publicized sufficiently, a special event can attract people from a wide area and contribute immeasurably to the profile of the community.

Through general promotional programs a town projects the image that it is an interesting place to shop and to visit. The tools for such promotional campaigns include slogans and logos, printed shopping bags, T-shirts, balloons, or bumper stickers, an awards system for best store windows, and events calendars. Promoting one's town in general terms is a year-round effort and should be budgeted for accordingly.

When planning an activities schedule, the co-ordinator must review and evaluate previous events. Unsuccessful past activities should be dropped and proven ones strengthened. Sponsorship should remain with the organizations that have traditionally organized each event. If they require assistance, encourage co-sponsorship. Decide on the number of events to be sponsored for the year, and design the schedule to accommodate activities that fall into each of the three categories of promotions. Brainstorm sessions are useful in preparing a list of ideas that could be accommodated within each promotion. The list should then be refined; facilities should be booked well in advance, and, wherever possible, conflicts with other community activities should be avoided. It is a useful idea to establish an events committee, lay out a plan of action, and delegate tasks. The most enthusiastic individuals should be encouraged to become involved in areas where they would contribute

The Sidewalk Days celebration in Moose Jaw, Saskatchewan, involves the whole region, including the local military base.

Standard ammunition in the campaign to promote downtown Perth, Ontario

The main highway west in southern Alberta draws tourist traffic to the recreated fort on the left, but bypasses Twenty-fourth Street – Fort Macleod's main street – on the right. The community has learned that it must reinforce the initial attraction of the fort with a wide range of recreational and cultural activities if it is to convince visitors to stop for long.

the most. Professionals and skilled persons should be recruited for leadership of key committees. The local media should also be kept abreast of the events committee's activities.

Budget

It is important that the project co-ordinator realize the financial necessities of promotion. A first-run event is especially difficult to budget; new ventures should be introduced on a scale that the organization can handle. Budget items might include:

1 Advertising: print and electronic media, handbills, posters, flyers, postage, banners, balloons, decals, bumper stickers
2 Equipment: sound, lighting, scaffolding; is it to be rental or purchase – that is, how often is it to be reused?
3 Facility rental: meeting-rooms
4 Food purchases for volunteers
5 Transportation
6 Clean-up
7 Special gimmicks: helium for balloons, horse-drawn haywagons, and so on
8 Entertainers' fees

When preparing a budget, show figures in the budget sheet for donated goods and services and labour. This can be useful for grant applications, since many agencies will give up to two-thirds of the costs if it can be demonstrated that other sources are being drawn upon. A meeting-room, even if donated, has a rental-equivalent value and should be acknowledged as such. Such donated materials and time show that the community is contributing something. It is only through trial and error that budgets, particularly advertising costs, can be fine-tuned to reflect the financial constraints of an organization.

Funds may be raised through voluntary business donations (either cash or goods or services), special-event grants, a yearly business contribution (as in the case of business-improvement areas), and service organizations. In a small town a cost-sharing approach seems most workable. Fund-raising may be more successful if fifty small businesses are asked to donate twenty-five dollars than if ten large ones are asked to contribute one hundred dollars each. The targeted total budget should be determined and then reasonable donations requested from all businesses and clubs throughout the community. Fund-raising in this manner is a more time-consuming task but a more successful way of raising funds, goods, or services. This method also involves more people as participants in the project and builds community pride. After an

Waiting for Santa in Cambridge, Ontario

event it is essential to thank all those who assisted and to give credit publicly to those who were instrumental in the success of the event.

Tourism

Tourism is important for job creation and community self-esteem. It is estimated that for every thirty thousand dollars spent in a community, one new job is created. The tourist dollar is an elusive one, however, and a successful strategy to attract tourists can be devised only by input from civic leaders, retail merchants, and the food, service, and accommodation sectors of the local economy. Most communities ignore the tourist-trade potential, catering instead to the traditional market, the local customers. For reasons of fiscal restraint or because they are unfamiliar with tourist needs, many small towns are unable to offer anything more than basic services to travellers.

Tourists are seldom attracted to a town on the strength of its retail section alone. Museums and historic sites attract tourists. So do cultural events, particularly the performing arts or special festivals displaying local crafts and talents. Recreational activities, particularly tournaments, winter and summer regional games, and special shows or fairs, can also bring people to town. Cultural activities remain the most consistent attraction for the tourist. In order to compete for the tourist dollar, small towns should organize a tourist-development body and plan and promote a series of events for the tourist season. Statistics on tourist travel and shopping patterns are available from federal and provincial departments, and these, along with local statistics, are essential to devising a strategy for attracting tourism.

If the community has convinced the traveller to detour from his intended destination, it must be able to capitalize on that impulse. If there are no interesting restaurants, or shops that sell books or pamphlets on the local area and its history, or nice places to stay the night, then the tourist will not stay long, nor will he spread his recommendations to friends. Fort Macleod has a proven tourist attraction in the Parks Canada replica of the original 1874 North-West Mounted Police fort, a facility that is host to more than fifty thousand visitors a year. Fewer than 5 per cent of those visitors, however, were finding their way to the town's Main Street, one block away. In the summer of 1983 a summer-theatre project was initiated which featured old-fashioned melodramas based on the town's history. This was attended by more than two thousand tourists. A student worker acted as a town-information source and walking-tour guide and promoted the downtown to an additional three thousand visitors. These efforts increased the traffic flow by 5 per cent, to double that of the previous year. Downtown business near the theatre reported an increase in tourist trade for summer 1983. It is obvious, however, that a tourist strategy can be considered success-ful only after a number of years. A similar NWMP post, British Columbia's Fort Steele, took eleven years to develop and consolidate its tourist base.

JACQUES DALIBARD

Epilogue

At the end of the children's classic *The Wizard of Oz*, Dorothy and her friends learn that their problems cannot be resolved by far-off magical powers. The answers to their problems, they discover, reside within. That conclusion, of course, is a cliché. But it also happens, very often, to be true. It is certainly a truth, as merchants on Main Street are beginning to realize, that applies to themselves.

When the traditional business heart of our communities was beset by problems, there was a tendency, at first, to go in search of magical solutions. A great deal of money was consequently spent imposing ideas from without. The result was everything from tacked-on theme villages to unnecessary street furniture to self-defeating downtown malls. Most of these solutions turned out to be quick fixes: they were arbitrary; they were gratuitous; they were expensive. They did not work.

What has been shown to work is the kind of Main Street approach described in this book. This approach is really quite modest. All it asks is that we look at Main Street's problems with common sense. It suggests that, before expensive plans are imposed from without, a few basic questions be asked: What exactly is a Main Street? What does it do? What does it offer? Why was it successful for so long? What is there on Main Street that, tapped, could bring new life to downtown Canada?

The answers to those questions are now largely known. And knowing them has led to a number of Main Street self-help programs that are both inexpensive and workable. The trick is to realize, as Dorothy did, that there is no place like home: all of the resources Main Street needs are already there, waiting to be used. The answers to Main Street's problems are on the doorstep.

References

Advisory Council on Historic Preservation *The Contribution of Historic Preservation to Urban Revitalization* Washington 1979

Alexander, L.A., ed *Downtown Mall Annual and Urban Design Report*. Vol 4. New York: Downtown Research and Development Center 1978

Almeras, J., et al *La forêt urbaine: cahier 1* Ville de Québec 1981

Anderson, L.O. *Wood Frame House Construction* Department of Agriculture handbook no 73. Washington, DC: U.S. Government Printing Office 1970

Anderson, Stanford, ed *On Streets* Cambridge, Mass: MIT Press 1978

Appleyard, D. *Livable Streets* Berkeley: University of California Press 1981

Artibise, A., and G. Stelter *Canada's Urban Past: A Bibliography to 1980 and Guide to Canadian Urban Studies* Vancouver: University of British Columbia Press 1981

Bartram, A. *Fascia Lettering in the British Isles* New York: Watson-Guptill Publications 1978

Bell, G., et al *Urban Environments and Human Behaviour: An Annotated Bibliography* Stroudsberg, Penn: Dowden, Hutchison & Ross 1973

Berk, E. *Downtown Improvement Manual* Chicago: American Society of Planning Officials 1976

Blumenson, J. *Identifying American Architecture: A Pictorial Guide to Style and Terms, 1600–1945* Nashville: American Association for State and Local History 1977

Boston Redevelopment Authority *City Signs and Lights: A Policy Study* Boston: MIT Press 1973

Brambilla, R., and G. Longo *For Pedestrians Only: Planning, Design, and Management of Traffic-Free Zones* New York: Whitney Library of Design 1977

Bryant, R.W.G. *Land: Private Property and Public Control* Montreal: Harvest House 1972

Bullock, O.M. Jr *The Restoration Manual* Norwalk, Conn: Silvermine Publishers 1966

Burkart, A. *Tourism: Past, Present and Future* London: Heineman Publishing 1974

Burns, J. *Connections: Ways to Discover and Realize Community Potentials* New York: McGraw-Hill 1979

Burton, T.L., et al *Guidelines for Urban Open Space Planning* Vanier: Canadian Parks / Recreation Association 1977

Byers, G.L., and H.E. Teckert *Marketing for Small Business: What It Is and Why You Need It* Toronto: Macmillan of Canada 1980

Byrne, R.O. *Conservation and Architectural Supply Sources and Brief Bibliographies* Ottawa: Association for Preservation Technology 1980

Canada, Federal Business Development Bank *Minding Your Own Business.* Vol 1. Montreal 1974

– *Minding Your Own Business.* Vol 2. Montreal 1980

Canada, Ministry of State, Urban Affairs *Directory of Canadian Urban Information Sources, 1977* Ottawa: Minister of Supply and Services Canada 1977

Cantacuzino, S. *New Uses for Old Buildings* London: Architectural Press 1975

Carson, A., and R. Dunlop *Inspecting a House* Toronto: General Publishing 1982

Cassidy, R. *Livable Cities: A Grass Roots Guide to Rebuilding Urban America* New York: Holt, Rinehart and Winston 1980

Ching, F.D.K. *Building Construction Illustrated* New York: Van Nostrand Reinhold 1977

Civic Trust *Pride of Place* London 1972

Colborne, R. *Fundamentals of Merchandise Presentation* Cincinnati: ST Publications 1982

Conseil International des Monuments et des Sites *Construire en quartier ancien* Paris: Ministère de l'Environnement et du Cadre de Vie 1980

Cutler, L. and S. *Recycling Cities for People: The Urban Design Process.* 2nd edn. Boston: CBI Publishing 1982

Dean, J. *Architectural Photography* Nashville: American Association for State and Local History 1981

Denhez, M. *Heritage Fights Back* Toronto: Heritage Canada and Fitzhenry & Whiteside 1978

Dumas, Antoine *A l'enseigne d'antan* Québec: Editions du Pélican 1970

Eldridge, H.J. *Common Defects in Buildings* London: Her Majesty's Stationery Office 1976

Emory, Michael *Windows* Chicago: Contemporary Books 1977

Evans, B., and A. Lawson *Shopfronts* New York: Van Nostrand Reinhold 1981

Federation of Canadian Municipalities *Management and Planning Capabilities in Small Communities* Ottawa 1982

Fitch, J.M. *Historic Preservation: Curatorial Management of the Built World* New York: McGraw-Hill 1982

Fleming, R.L. *Façade Stories: Changing Faces of Main Street Storefronts and How to Care for Them* New York: Hastings House Publishers 1982

Fleming, R.L., et al *On Common Ground: Caring for Shared Land from Town Common to Urban Green* Boston: Harvard University Press 1982

Fulweilder, J.H. *How to Promote Your Shopping Center* New York: Chain Store Age Books 1973

Galambos, E.C., and A.F. Schreiber *Making Sense out of Dollars: Economic Analysis for Local Government* Washington: National League of Cities 1978

Gowans, A. *Building Canada: An Architectural History of Canadian Life* Toronto: Oxford University Press 1966

Gunn, C. *Tourism Planning* New York: Crane and Russack 1979

Guthrie, Susan *Main Street Historic District: Van Burken, Arkansas.* Preservation Case Studies. Washington: Technical Preservation Services, HCRS, U.S. Dept of the Interior 1980

Harris, C.M., ed *Dictionary of Architecture and Construction* New York: McGraw-Hill 1975

– *Illustrated Dictionary of Historic Architecture.* Reprint. New York: McGraw-Hill 1977. Originally published as *Historic Architecture Sourcebook* New York: Dover Publications 1973

Hearn, J. *The Canadian Old House Catalogue* Toronto: Van Nostrand Reinhold 1980

Heritage Canada *Commercial Signage Manual* Ottawa 1985

– *Public Improvements: A Training Manual for Use by Public Officials* Ottawa 1985

– *Window Display Manual* Ottawa 1985

Hornbeck, J.S., ed *Stores and Shopping Centers* New York: McGraw-Hill 1962

Hutchins, N. *Restoring Old Houses* Toronto: Van Nostrand Reinhold 1980

Joel, S. *Fairchild's Book of Window Display* New York: Fairchild Publications 1973

Kalman, H., et al *Encore: Recycling Public Buildings for the Arts* Don Mills, Ont: Corpus Information Services 1980

Kinnier, J. *Words and Buildings: The Art and Practice of Public Lettering* London: Architectural Press 1980

Litchfield, M.W. *Renovation: A Complete Guide* New York: John Wiley and Sons 1982

McCready, G.B. *Marketing Tactics Master Guide for Small Business* Englewood Cliffs, NJ: Prentice-Hall 1982

McKee, H.J., comp *Recording Historic Buildings* Washington: National Parks Service, Department of the Interior 1970

McNulty, R.H., and S.A. Climent, eds *Neighborhood Conservation: A Handbook of Methods and Techniques* New York: Whitney Library of Design 1976

Maddex, Diane, ed *New Energy from Old Buildings* Washington: National Trust for Historic Preservation 1981

Makuch, S.M. *Canadian Municipal and Planning Law* Toronto: Carswell 1983

Mang, Karl and Eva *New Shops* New York: Architectural Book Publishing 1982

Markowitz, A.L. *Historic Preservation: A Guide to Information Sources.* Art and Architecture Information Series, vol 13. Detroit: Gale Research Company 1980

Mun, David *Shops: A Manual of Planning and Design* London: Architectural Press 1981

National Trust for Historic Preservation *Old and New Architecture: Design Relationship* Washington: Preservation Press 1980

Organization for Economic Co-operation and Development *Streets for People* Paris 1974

Pegler, M.M., ed *Store Windows That Sell*. Vol II. New York: Retail Reporting Corp 1982

Pressman, N., et al *Creating Livable Cities* Waterloo, Ont: Faculty of Environmental Studies, University of Waterloo 1981

Ramati, Raquel *How to Save Your Own Street* Garden City, NY: Doubleday 1981

Rifkind, Carol *Main Street: The Face of Urban America* New York: Harper & Row, Harper Colophon Books 1978

Rosenow, J.E., and G.L. Pulsipher *Tourism: The Good, the Bad, and the Ugly* Lincoln, Neb: Century Three Press 1979

Sanoff, H., ed *Designing with Community Participation* New York: McGraw-Hill 1978

Schmertz, M.F., et al *New Life for Old Buildings* New York: McGraw-Hill 1982

Shaffer, H., and H. Greenwall *Independent Retailing: A Moneymaking Manual* Englewood Cliffs, NJ: Prentice-Hall 1976

Spielman, P. and S. *Alphabets and Design for Wood Signs*. Home Craftsman Series. New York: Sterling Publishing 1983

Steele, Fritz *The Sense of Place* Boston: CBI Publishing 1982

Tennessee Valley Authority *Townlift: Building Improvement Manual* Knoxville 1978

Thompson, E.K., ed *Recycling Buildings: Renovations, Remodelings, Restorations and Reuses* New York: McGraw-Hill 1977

Urban Land Institute and National Parking Congress *Dimensions of Parking* Washington 1979

Vancouver, City Planning Dept *Gastown Sign Guidelines* Vancouver 1974

Walsh, E. Denis, and associates *Action Plan, Southbridge, Massachusetts: The Renovation and Reuse of Upper Storey Space in an Older Downtown Commercial Building* Boston: Commonwealth of Massachusetts, Department of Community Affairs 1978

Warner, R.M., and S.M. Groff *Business and Preservation: A Survey of Business Conservation of Buildings and Neighborhoods* New York: Inform 1978

Whyte, W.H. *The Social Life of Small Urban Spaces* Washington: Conservation Foundation 1980

Wiedenhoeft, R. *Cities for People: Practical Measures for Improving Urban Environments* New York: Van Nostrand Reinhold 1981

Wingate, J.W., and S. Helfant *Small Store Planning for Growth*. 2nd edn. Small Business Management Series, no 33. Washington: Small Business Administration 1977

Ziegler, A.P. Jr, and W.C. Kidney *Historic Preservation in Small Towns: A Manual of Practice* Nashville: American Association for State and Local History 1980

Contributors

Pierre Berton, author and journalist, is a leading advocate of preservation. He was a member of the board of governors of the Heritage Canada Foundation from 1973 to 1983 and served as chairman of the board during the last five years of this term.

Jacques Dalibard, a recognized leader in restoration architecture, has been the executive director of the Heritage Canada Foundation since 1978. He is responsible for implementing the mandate of the foundation and for its overall operation, and has been the prime generating force behind Main Street Canada.

John Edwards was a research architect with the Heritage Canada Foundation and is now in private practice in Perth, Ontario.

Gordon Fulton is assistant director for Operations and Management of Heritage Canada's Main Street program. He was previously Main Street co-ordinator in Moose Jaw, Saskatchewan.

Deryck Holdsworth is assistant editor of volume 3 of the *Historical Atlas of Canada* and has written articles on Canadian regional architecture and historic preservation.

Hans Honegger is assistant director for Design of Heritage Canada's Main Street program. He was previously Main Street co-ordinator in Nelson, British Columbia.

Peter Hyndman is the Atlantic regional co-ordinator for Heritage Canada's Main Street program. He was previously the architect for both the Windsor and Bridgetown, Nova Scotia, Main Street projects and co-ordinator in Bridgetown.

Robert Inwood is Downtown Development officer for the City of Nelson, British Columbia.

Harold Kalman is a consultant in the history and conservation of architecture, with a national practice based in Ottawa. He is the author of numerous books, including *The Railway Hotels* (1968), *Exploring Vancouver* (1974), *The Sensible Rehabilitation of Older Houses* (1979), *Encore: Recycling Public Buildings for the Arts* (1980), and *Exploring Ottawa* (1983).

Don Macintosh, Main Street co-ordinator for Cambridge, Ontario, has previously worked as a landscape architect.

Jim Mountain is Western regional co-ordinator for Heritage Canada's Main Street program. He was previously Main Street co-ordinator in Fort Macleod, Alberta.

Chris Pelham, Main Street co-ordinator for Windsor, Nova Scotia, has worked as a property manager for Heritage Canada and the City of Halifax.

John Stewart, director of the Heritage Canada Foundation's Main Street program from 1980 to 1984, is now an architect in private practice in Perth, Ontario.

Picture Credits

References are to the pages on which illustrations from each credited source appear.

Architectural Record 160
David Thompson University Archives 16 (bottom), 34, 35 (top)
Glenbow-Alberta Archives 152, 222, 226 (top)
Hants Journal 157 (top)
Master's Studio, Leamington, Ontario 155 (bottom)
Moose Jaw Public Library Archives 62
Nelson *Daily News* 6
Norwich Revitalization Plan Manual 67
City of St John's 155 (top)
Saskatchewan Archives Board 158 (top) RA-888(4); 166 Alan Vanstone Collection R-Pl 587, printed with permission of the donor, Mrs G. Helen Vanstone
Vancouver Public Library 158 (bottom) Timms Collection photo 5222
F.W. Woolworth Co 26

Jan Douglas 220
John Edwards 74, 78
Art Ferrari 192
Gordon Fulton 79, 88, 122, 161, 162, 163, 168, 170, 171, 175, 178, 202, 215, 231
Deryck Holdsworth 39, 70
Hans Honegger 10 (top), 35 (bottom), 56, 84, 86, 87, 98, 102 (top right and left), 103 (top), 104, 105, 107, 116, 119, 120, 121 (bottom), 124, 126, 127, 132, 133 (bottom), 134, 135, 136, 137, 138 (top), 138 (drawing by Hans Honegger), 139 (top right), 150, 176, 177, 195, 206

Peter Hyndman 82, 89, 108, 130, 188, 189, 225 (top)
Robert Inwood 103 (bottom), 133 (top), 147, 148, 149, 169
Harold Kalman 9, 10 (bottom), 11, 12, 16 (top), 20, 21, 22 (bottom), 33, 47, 51,
    53, 70, 73 (top), 81 (top), 187, 196, 197
Stuart Lazear 92, 121 (top)
Don Macintosh 30, 90 (top), 128, 181, 199, 209, 234
Shawn MacKenzie 113, 140, 141, 212, 232 (top)
Cheryl Moss 201, 214
Jim Mountain 27, 68, 111, 223, 225 (bottom), 226 (bottom), 228, 232 (bottom)
Scott Smith 191, 194
Art Stevens 102 (bottom), 146
John Stewart 81 (bottom), 112, 165
Herb Stovel 90 (bottom), 139 (top left, bottom)
François Varin 2
Martin Weaver 41 (bottom)